LATIN LANGUAGE TESTS
for Levels 1, 2 and GCSE

Ashley Carter

Bristol Classical Press

First published in 2011 by
Bristol Classical Press
an imprint of
Bloomsbury Academic
Bloomsbury Publishing Plc
36 Soho Square,
London W1D 3QY, UK

CIP records for this book are available from the
British Library and the Library of Congress

ISBN 978-1-85399-749-5

Typeset by Ashley Carter
Printed and bound in Great Britain by
CPI Antony Rowe, Chippenham and Eastbourne

www.bloomsburyacademic.com

Contents

Introduction for the Teacher

This book of unprepared translation and comprehension tests has been designed to help teachers to prepare their students for the language units in the two new Latin specifications: WJEC's Levels 1 and 2 and OCR's GCSE. The Level 1 units cover broadly the same range of linguistic material as GCSE Foundation Tier, while the Level 2 units equate to GCSE Higher Tier.

Despite their basic similarity, the two specifications differ in their detail: the defined vocabulary lists attached to each unit are not quite the same; the list of included accidence and syntax varies from unit to unit, apart from the most demanding units from each specification, which are almost identical. The units also differ in format, with varying proportions of comprehension and translation and different word-counts. Whereas the OCR comprehension questions are broadly traditional in style, those of WJEC are rather more adventurous.

These differences are sufficient to call for a separate series of tests for each unit of the two specifications, apart from A402 and 9524, which are so similar in form and content that a single series should suffice for both. All the tests have been modelled as closely as possible on the published specifications and sample assessment materials, including past papers. The aim has been to provide students with tests that approximate as closely as possible to the real thing, so that when they take the examinations, there will be no surprises. Teachers should also have a reliable and accurate tool for assessing progress.

For reasons of space, the layout of the tests differs from that used in live examinations, for the simple reason that all public examinations at these levels are obliged to provide space for answers on the question papers. In a book that will be reused, this would not be appropriate.

Mark schemes are available for every test, and may be purchased from the publisher in the form of a separate booklet, *Latin Language Tests: Mark Schemes*. These schemes are also based as closely as possible on those used in live examinations. Teachers should be aware, however, that, in the light of experience, the examination boards are likely to reassess periodically the usefulness of the schemes originally adopted. It must also be remembered that mark schemes tend to contain only one of several, sometimes many, possible answers; teachers must use their discretion in determining whether particular answers should be accepted or not.

The author is indebted to Alan Clague for all the advice and suggestions he offered during the compilation of this book, and especially for checking the accuracy of the Latin.

A Note to the Student

Please remember to make your answers legible; if an Examiner can't read what you write, s/he won't be able to give you the mark. In translations, check that you have written something for every Latin word, using guesswork if you don't know a word. Remember that a guess may be close enough to gain some credit, whereas a blank space can earn no marks at all.

You will find that most questions start with some Latin words in italics. An example from the very first test is *'Clemens ... Septimus* (lines 1-2): who was Septimus?'. The two Latin words in italics are intended to direct you to the part of the story where you will find the answer. Unless the question is clearly asking you to look elsewhere, you should always confine your answer to what is inside these quoted words.

Please note that proper names are glossed only the first time they appear and are not underlined here, though in real examination papers they usually are. Remember that all proper names should be rendered in English in the nominative case. All underlined words are glossed beneath the passage.

Section 1. Tests for WJEC Level 1 Core

Introduction

These tests contain 70% comprehension questions and 30% translation, split into short sentences or phrases. The storylines all relate to some aspect of daily life, and are entirely imaginary. There is usually a slight gradient of difficulty, with simpler sentences at the start and more challenging Latin and questions towards the end.

The mark schemes generally allocate one mark for every Latin word that forms part of the answer, whether in the form of comprehension or translation. Exceptions to this are when glossed or repeated words are included: these often carry no separate mark; similarly there is no separate mark in comprehension answers for prepositions: these are regarded as forming a unit of sense in combination with their dependent nouns.

Confusion between singular and plural nouns and verbs is one of the commonest sources of error in these tests. Students should be advised to pay particular attention to these.

1 *Clemens takes his son on his first visit to the baths. The activities of a family slave, however, cause problems.*

1 Claudia erat filia Clementis. Clemens filium quoque habebat; nomen
2 eius erat Septimus. olim Clemens Septimo dixit, 'volo te hodie mecum
3 venire. iam tempus est tibi ad thermas ire, quod iuvenis es, non puer.'
4 Septimus laetus erat, quod numquam antea thermas intraverat.
5 Claudia tamen, 'sed pater,' inquit, 'ego quoque volo thermas visitare.
6 nonne vobiscum venire possum?' 'non potes, filia,' respondit Clemens.
7 'si tu thermas videre vis, necesse est tibi cum matre ire. ego solos
8 iuvenes in thermas ducere possum.'
9   mox Septimus et pater laete e domo discesserunt. servus quoque
10 ibat, oleum et strigiles portans. multi alii cives per vias urbis iter
11 faciebant. thermae, ad quas omnes festinabant, maximae erant. ubi
12 intraverunt, Septimus attonitus erat, quod palaestra erat plena
13 hominum currentium clamantiumque. Clemens filium in apodyterium
14 duxit. vestes servo tradiderunt; ille eas custodiebat. postquam in
15 tepidario paulisper sederunt, caldarium intraverunt, sed Septimus
16 celeriter exiit, quod difficile ei erat calorem tolerare. pater risit.
17 postquam frigidarium intraverunt, Septimus in aquam laetus desiluit.
18   tandem Clemens Septimo dixit, 'nunc discedere debemus; mater
19 tua nos exspectat.' ubi in apodyterium redierunt, vestes quaerebant;
20 sed eas videre non poterant. servus, qui vestes custodiverat, aberat.
21 Clemens iratissimus erat. ei necesse erat novas tunicas emere.
22 simulatque e thermis exierunt, Clemens uxorem et filiam conspexit.
23 'quid vos facitis?' inquit Clemens attonitus. 'in thermis fuimus,'
24 respondit uxor. 'laetissimae sumus,' inquit Claudia, 'quod in thermis
25 servus noster anulum aureum invenit. servus mihi eum dedit. ecce!
26 nonne anulus pulcher est?' 'vos estis felices,' dixit Clemens, 'sed ubi
27 est servus?' 'ego eum ad tabernam misi,' respondit uxor. iam Clemens
28 erat etiam iratior.

Names

Claudia, -ae f.	Claudia	*Clemens, -entis* m.	Clemens
Septimus, -i m.	Septimus		

Words

nomen, -inis n.	name	*si*	if
tempus, -oris n.	time	*necesse*	necessary
thermae, -arum f.pl.	baths	*oleum, -i* n.	oil
antea	before	*strigilis, -is* f.	strigil (for
visito, -are	I visit		scraping oil)
vobiscum	with you	*attonitus, -a, -um*	astonished

palaestra, -ae f.	exercise area	*frigidarium, -i* n.	cold room
plenus, -a, -um	full	*desilio, -ire, -ui*	I jump down
apodyterium, -i n.	changing room	*absum, -esse*	I am missing
vestes, -ium f.pl.	clothes	*tunica, -ae* f.	tunic
custodio, -ire, -ivi	I guard	*emo, -ere*	I buy
tepidarium, -i n.	warm room	*anulus, -i* m.	ring
paulisper	for a short time	*aureus, -a, -um*	gold
caldarium, -i n.	hot room	*invenio, -ire, -veni*	I find
calor, -oris m.	heat	*ecce!*	look!
tolero, -are	I bear, stand	*felix, -icis*	lucky

1 Who was Claudia (line 1) [2]

2 *Clemens ... Septimus* (lines 1-2): who was
   Septimus? [1]

3 Which is the correct translation of *olim
   Clemens Septimo dixit* (line 2)?
       A when Clemens said to Septimus
       B once Clemens said to Septimus
       C when Septimus said to Clemens
       D once Septimus said to Clemens [1]

4 Translate *volo te hodie mecum venire* (lines 2-3). [5]

5 *iam ... puer* (line 3): which **two** of the following statements are true?
   Write down the letters for the ones that are correct.
       A it was time for Septimus to go to the baths
       B it was time for Clemens to go to the baths
       C Septimus was a young man, not a boy
       D Septimus was a boy, not a young man [2]

6 *Septimus ... intraverat* (line 4): why was Septimus happy? [3]

7 *Claudia ... possum* (lines 5-6):
       (i)   to whom did Claudia speak? [1]
       (ii)   what did Claudia want to do? [1]
       (iii) what did she ask her father? [3]

8 Write down and translate the **two** Latin words in line 6 that answer
   Claudia's request. [2]

9 *si ... possum* (lines 7-8):
       (i)   what did Clemens say Claudia ought to do if she wanted to see
            the baths? [2]

(ii) what reason did Clemens give for telling her this? [4]

10 Translate *mox ... discesserunt* (line 9). [6]

11 *servus ... portans* (lines 9-10):
    (i) who accompanied Septimus and Clemens? [1]
    (ii) what was this person doing? [2]

12 *multi ... erant* (lines 10-11):
    (i) who were hurrying through the streets? [3]
    (ii) where were they going? [1]
    (iii) write down and translate the Latin word that describes
    thermas. [2]

13 *ubi ... clamantiumque* (lines 11-13): which **four** of the following
statements are true? Write down the letters for the ones that are correct.
    A they entered the city
    B they entered the baths
    C Septimus was astonished
    D Septimus astonished his father
    E there were no people in the exercise area
    F there were many people in the exercise area
    G Septimus was running and shouting
    H people were running and shouting [4]

14 *Clemens ... custodiebat* (lines 13-14):
    (i) what did Clemens and Septimus do when they entered the
    changing room? [3]
    (ii) why did they do that? [1]

15 *postquam ... sederunt* (lines 14-15): what did Clemens and
Septimus do in the warm room? [1]

16 *caldarium ... tolerare* (lines 15-16):
    (i) what did Septimus do after entering the hot room? [2]
    (ii) why did he do this? [2]

17 Which is the correct translation of *pater risit* (line 16)?
    A he laughed at his father
    B he was laughing at his father
    C his father was laughing
    D his father laughed [1]

18 *postquam ... desiluit* (line 17): what did Septimus do in the
cold room? [2]

19 Translate *tandem ... exspectat* (lines 18-19). [11]

20 *ubi ... aberat* (lines 19-20): describe fully what happened when
   Clemens and Septimus returned to the changing room. [7]

21 Translate *Clemens iratissimus erat* (line 21). [3]

22 *ei ... emere* (line 21): what did Clemens say he would have to do? [2]

23 *simulatque ... conspexit* (line 22): what happened as soon as they
   left the baths? [4]

24 Translate *quid vos facitis* (line 23). [3]

25 Which is the correct translation of *in thermis fuimus* (line 23)?
   A   we were visiting the baths
   B   we went into the baths
   C   we have been in the baths
   D   we swam in the baths [1]

26 *laetissimae ... dedit* (lines 24-25): which **two** of the following statements
   are true? Write down the letters for the ones that are correct.
   A   the women were very happy
   B   the men were very happy
   C   their slave had found a ring and given it to Claudia
   D   they had lost a ring but the slave found it [2]

27 Write down and translate the Latin word in line 26 that describes
   the ring. [2]

28 In lines 26-27, what did Clemens ask his wife? [2]

29 *ego ... iratior* (lines 27-28):
   (i)   what was the wife's answer? [2]
   (ii) how did Clemens react to her answer? [3]

Total [100]

2   *Helen helps her friend to gain a better life.*

1 Helena in pulchra <u>villa</u> habitabat. pater Helenae multos servos, multas
2 ancillas habebat. inter ancillas erat puella, Phoebe. quamquam
3 Phoebe in domo laborare debebat, Helena et Phoebe erant <u>amicae</u>;
4 saepe ad tabernas ibant, multaque alia <u>una</u> faciebant. quod Helena
5 erat puella, ad <u>ludum</u> cum <u>fratribus</u> non ibat. pater eius, qui vir <u>dives</u>
6 erat, <u>iusserat</u> unum ex servis eam <u>docere</u>. hic servus, Hyacinthus,
7 legere poterat. olim Helena patri dixit: 'cur Hyacinthus Phoeben
8 mecum non <u>docet</u>? Phoebe <u>intellegens</u> est. ancilla <u>docta</u> maiorem
9 <u>valorem</u> habet.' pater, quod filiam amabat, <u>consensit</u>.
10   itaque per tres <u>annos</u> Hyacinthus duas puellas <u>litteras</u> <u>numerosque</u>
11 <u>docebat</u>. tandem Phoebe intellegebat omnia quae Hyacinthus <u>sciebat</u>;
12 sed non erat laeta, nam etiam nunc domum <u>purgare</u> debebat. olim
13 Phoebe <u>aberat</u>; <u>necesse</u> erat <u>ceteris</u> ancillis facere ea quae Phoebe
14 facere <u>solebat</u>. illae iratissimae erant et laborare nolebant. pater
15 Helenam <u>iussit</u> <u>amicam</u> quaerere. ubi Helena eam tandem conspexit in
16 horto sedentem, 'cur,' inquit, 'tu non laboras? pater meus est iratus.'
17 'non laboro,' Phoebe respondit, 'quod iam legere et scribere et
18 <u>numerare</u> possum. sed iam <u>vita</u> mea <u>peior</u> est quam <u>antea</u>.'
19   Helena, quae <u>anxia</u> erat, ad patrem festinavit. ei narravit ea quae
20 Phoebe dixerat. pater, postquam hoc audivit, etiam iratior erat, quod
21 servos <u>ignavos</u> habere nolebat. 'pater <u>carissime</u>,' inquit Helena,
22 <u>manum</u> patris tenens, 'nonne Phoebe <u>docta</u> est? tibi <u>necesse</u> est ei
23 <u>laborem</u> meliorem dare. num crudelis esse vis?' Helena <u>suaviter</u>
24 ridebat. quid aliud pater facere potuit? mox, ubi pater amicis cenam
25 dabat, Phoebe <u>versus</u> <u>recitabat</u>. pater iam laetus erat, quod omnes
26 amici eam laudabant. Helena et Phoebe quoque erant laetae.

Names

Helena, -ae f.	Helena	*Phoebe, -es* f. (acc. *-en*)	Phoebe
Hyacinthus, -i m.	Hyacinthus		

Words

villa, -ae f.	house	*doctus, -a, -um*	educated
amica, -ae f.	friend	*valor, -oris* m.	value
una	together	*consentio –ire, -sensi*	I agree
ludus, -i m.	school	*annus, -i* m.	year
frater, -ris m.	brother	*littera, -ae* f.	letter
dives, -itis	rich	*numerus, -i* m.	number
iubeo, -ere, iussi	I order	*scio, -ire*	I know
doceo, -ere	I teach	*purgo, -are*	I clean
intellegens, -ntis	intelligent		

absum, -esse	I am missing	*anxius, -a, -um*	anxious
necesse	necessary	*ignavus, -a, -um*	idle
ceteri, -ae, -a	the rest (of)	*carus, -a, -um*	dear
soleo, -ere	I am accustomed	*manus, -us* f.	hand
numero, -are	I count	*labor, -oris* m.	work
vita, -ae f.	life	*suaviter*	sweetly
peior, -ius	worse	*versus* (acc. pl. *–us*)	poem
antea	before	*recito, -are*	I recite

1   *Helena ... habitabat* (line 1): what information are we given about
    Helena?   [2]

2   *pater ... habebat* (lines 1-2): what did Helena's father have?   [3]

3   *inter ... Phoebe* (line 2): give two details about Phoebe.   [2]

4   *quamquam ... amicae* (lines 2-3): which **three of** the following
    statements are true? Write down the letters for the ones that are
    correct.
    A   Phoebe worked in the house
    B   Helena had to work in the house
    C   Phoebe had to work
    D   Phoebe owed her master work
    E   Helena and Phoebe had some friends
    F   Helena and Phoebe were friends   [3]

5   Translate *saepe ... faciebant* (line 4).   [7]

6   *quod ... ibat* (lines 4-5):
    (i)   what did Helena not do?   [3]
    (ii) what reason is given for this?   [1]

7   *pater ... docere* (lines 5-6):
    (i)   write down the Latin adjective that describes Helena's father.   [1]
    (ii) what order had he given?   [3]

8   *hic servus legere poterat* (lines 6-7): which is the correct translation
    of these words?
    A   the slave could choose this
    B   the slave could read this
    C   this slave could choose
    D   this slave could read   [1]

9   Translate *olim ... docet* (lines 7-8).   [9]

15

10 *Phoebe ... habet* (lines 8-9): what arguments does Helena use to try to persuade her father? [3]

11 *pater ... consensit* (line 9): why did Helena's father agree? [2]

12 *itaque ... docebat* (lines 10-11): which **three** of the following statements are true? Write down the letters for the ones that are correct.
    A   Hyacinthus taught three girls
    B   Hyacinthus taught two girls
    C   Hyacynthus taught for three years
    D   Hyacinthus taught for two years
    E   the girls were taught to read and count
    F   the girls sent large numbers of letters [3]

13 *tandem ... sciebat* (line 11): what did Phoebe at last understand? [3]

14 *sed ... debebat* (line 12): why was Phoebe unhappy? [3]

15 *necesse ... solebat* (lines 13-14): what happened when Phoebe went missing? [4]

16 Translate *illae iratissimae erant et laborare nolebant* (line 14). [5]

17 Which is the correct translation of *pater Helenam iussit amicam quaerere* (lines 14-15)?
    A   Helena's father ordered her friend to search
    B   Helena's father ordered her to search her friend
    C   Helena's father ordered her to search for her friend
    D   Helena ordered her father to search for her friend [1]

18 *ubi ... iratus* (lines 15-16):
    (i)   where was Phoebe? [1]
    (ii)   what was she doing there? [1]
    (iii) what question did Helena ask her? [2]
    (iv) what did she say about her father? [1]

19 *non laboro ... antea* (lines 17-18): explain in your own words why Phoebe did not want to work. [4]

20 *Helena ... dixerat* (lines 19-20): what two things did Helena do? [5]

21 Translate *pater ... nolebat* (lines 20-21). [11]

22 *pater ... est* (lines 21-22):
    (i)   which word best describes Helena's actions and words? Write down your chosen letter **and** give a reason for your answer.
        A coaxing
        B anxious
        C angry
        D hostile   [1]

    (ii)   which is the correct translation of *nonne Phoebe docta est*?
        A Phoebe isn't educated, is she?
        B is Phoebe educated?
        C is Phoebe educated, or isn't she?
        D Phoebe is educated, isn't she?   [1]

23 *tibi ... vis* (lines 22-23):
    (i)   what did Helena say her father should do?   [2]
    (ii)   what impression does she **not** want her father to give?   [1]

24 *Helena ... potuit* (lines 23-24):
    (i)   why do you think Helena smiled sweetly?   [1]
    (ii)   how do we know that Helena was successful?   [1]

25 *mox ... recitabat* (lines 24-25):
    (i)   what did Phoebe now do to help Helena's father?   [1]
    (ii)   when did she do this?   [4]

26 *pater ... laetae* (lines 25-26):
    (i)   what happened to make Helena's father feel *laetus*?   [3]
    (ii)   how did Helena and Phoebe now feel?   [1]

Total [100]

3   *A gladiator loses a contest and is persuaded to retire.*

1 Musculus erat gladiator. Musculus in ludo prope mediam urbem
2 habitabat. in ludo omnes gladiatores cenabant, se exercebant et
3 dormiebant. Musculus erat vir fortis sed parvus. nomen 'Musculum'
4 habebat, quod saepe in pugnis sub gladios adversariorum celeriter
5 currebat et eos necabat. Musculus multos adversarios superaverat.
6 cives igitur eum amabant. ubi Musculus per vias urbis ambulabat, viri
7 et feminae eum salutabant.
8   olim senator munus dabat. inter gladiatores erat Musculus.
9 Musculus laetus erat, quod semper pugnare volebat. adversarius eius
10 tamen erat Scorpus, vir ingens et crudelis, qui multas victorias iam
11 habebat. pugna difficilis fuit: Scorpus Musculum bene intellegebat,
12 quod in arena eum saepe spectaverat. Musculus, quamquam celerior
13 erat quam Scorpus, eum superare non potuit. tandem Musculus erat
14 fessus. Scorpus gladium e manu eius pepulit. sine gladio Musculus
15 vincere non potuit. subito Scorpus Musculum ad terram pepulit.
16 Scorpus super corpus Musculi stetit, gladium ad guttur tenens. paratus
17 erat eum necare. senator, postquam hoc conspexit, turbam
18 spectatorum spectavit. illi mortem Musculi nolebant. itaque senator
19 pollicem vertit. ubi Scorpus circum arenam ambulavit triumphans,
20 spectatores laete plauserunt. Musculus ex arena festinavit, laetus
21 quod etiam vivebat, sed tristis quod Scorpus eum superaverat.
22   postridie femina nobilis ad ludum venit. 'quid vis, domina?' inquit
23 servus, qui ad portam stabat. 'ego Musculo donum dare volo,'
24 respondit femina. servus feminam ad cellam Musculi duxit. illa statim,
25 'volo te emere,' inquit. 'heri, ubi Scorpus paratus erat te necare,
26 perterrita eram. nolo id iterum videre.' 'sed, domina,' Musculus dixit,
27 'gladiator sum; quid aliud facere possum?' 'ego tibi libertatem dare
28 volo,' femina dixit. 'deinde tu omnes servos in mea domo curare
29 potes.' Musculus erat laetus.

Names

Musculus, -i m.	Musculus	*Scorpus, -i* m.	Scorpus

Words

gladiator, -oris m.	gladiator	*sub* + acc.	under
ludus, -i m.	gladiatorial school	*gladius, -i* m.	sword
		adversarius, -i m.	opponent
ceno, -are	I eat a meal	*senator, -oris* m.	senator
se exercebant	(they) trained	*munus, -eris* n.	gladiatorial show
nomen, -inis n.	name	*victoria, -ae* f.	victory
pugna, -ae f.	fight, contest	*arena, -ae* f.	arena

fessus, -a, -um	tired	*circum* + acc.	round
e manu	from his hand	*triumphans, -antis*	triumphant
		plaudo, -ere, plausi	I applaud
pello, -ere, pepuli	I knock	*tristis, -is, -e*	sad
sine + abl.	without	*postridie*	the next day
vinco, -ere	I win	*nobilis, -is, -e*	noble
super + acc.	over	*cella, -ae* f.	cell, room
corpus, -oris n.	body	*emo, -ere*	I buy
guttur, -uris n.	throat	*iterum*	again
paratus, -a, -um	ready	*libertas, -atis* f.	freedom
turba, -ae f.	crowd	*curo, -are*	I take charge of
spectator, -oris m.	spectator		
pollicem verto, -ere, -i	I turn the thumb (to spare the defeated gladiator's life)		

1   *Musculus ... habitabat* (lines 1-2): where did Musculus live?   [4]

2   *in ludo ... dormiebant* (lines 2-3): what **three** things did the gladiators do?   [3]

3   Write down and translate the **two** Latin adjectives in line 3 that describe Musculus.   [4]

4   *nomen ... necabat* (lines 3-5): *Musculus* means 'Little Mouse'. Explain fully why Musculus was given this name.   [3]

5   *Musculus ... amabant* (lines 5-6):
     (i)   what had Musculus done?   [2]
     (ii) what was the result of this?   [2]

6   Translate *ubi ... salutabant* (lines 6-7).   [9]

7   *olim ... dabat* (line 8): what was the senator doing?   [2]

8   Which is the correct translation of *inter gladiatores erat Musculus* (line 8)?
          A   Musculus was among the gladiators
          B   Musculus was between the gladiators
          C   the gladiators were around Musculus
          D   he was between the gladiators and Musculus   [1]

9   *Musculus ... volebat* (line 9): why was Musculus happy?   [3]

10 *adversarius ... habebat* (lines 9-11): which **three** of the following statements are true? Write down the letters for the ones that are correct.

     A Musculus' opponent had defeated Scorpus
     B Musculus' opponent was Scorpus
     C Scorpus' opponent was a huge and cruel man
     D Scorpus was a huge and cruel man
     E Scorpus had won many victories
     F Scorpus' opponent had won many victories   [3]

11 Write down and translate the Latin word in line 11 that describes the fight.   [2]

12 *Scorpus ... spectaverat* (lines 11-12): why did Scorpus understand Musculus well?   [4]

13 Translate *Musculus ... potuit* (lines 12-13).   [9]

14 *tandem ... pepulit* (lines 13-14):
    (i) why was Scorpus able to defeat Musculus?   [1]
    (ii) how did he defeat him?   [2]

15 Which is the correct translation of *Musculus vincere non potuit* (lines 14-15)?
     A Musculus was not allowed to win
     B he could not defeat Musculus
     C Musculus did not expect to win
     D Musculus could not win   [1]

16 *stetit* (line 16): which is the correct meaning of this word?
     A he stands
     B he was standing
     C he stood
     D he had stood   [1]

17 *gladium ad guttur tenens* (line 16): how did Scorpus threaten Musculus?   [2]

18 *paratus ... necare* (lines 16-17): what was Scorpus ready to do?   [1]

19 *senator ... vertit* (lines 17-19):
    (i) why do you think the senator looked at the crowd of spectators?   [1]
    (ii) how did the crowd feel about the outcome of the fight?   [2]

20 *ubi ... plauserunt* (lines 19-20): which **three** of the following statements are true? Write down the letters for the ones that are correct.
    A Scorpus walked round the arena
    B Scorpus ran round the arena
    C the spectators were triumphant
    D Scorpus was triumphant
    E the spectators were happy
    F Scorpus was happy   [3]

21 *Musculus ... superaverat* (lines 20-21):
    (i)   what **two** feelings did Musculus have?   [2]
    (ii) why did he feel like this?   [2]

22 *postridie ... venit* (line 22): what happened the next day?   [3]

23 Translate *quid ... stabat* (lines 22-23).   [8]

24 *ego ... femina* (lines 23-24): what did the woman say she wanted to do?   [3]

25 *servus ... duxit* (line 24): what did the slave do?   [3]

26 *illa ... inquit* (lines 24-25): what did the woman say to Musculus?   [2]

27 *heri ... videre* (lines 25-26): which **three** of the following statements are true? Write down the letters for the ones that are correct.
    A yesterday the woman was terrified
    B Scorpus was terrified
    C yesterday Musculus was ready to kill Scorpus
    D Scorpus was ready to kill Musculus
    E the woman did not want to see it happen again
    F the woman did not want to see Musculus again   [3]

28 *sed ... possum* (lines 26-27): what do you think Musculus meant by these words?   [2]

29 Translate *ego tibi libertatem dare volo* (lines 27-28).   [4]

30 *deinde ... potes* (lines 28-29): what did the woman want Musculus to do?   [3]

Total [100]

4a *Sextus and Marcus are captured by pirates. Marcus' father goes to look for them.*

1 Sextus et Marcus erant amici et in <u>proximis</u> domibus habitabant.
2 <u>extra</u> urbem, ubi pueri habitabant, erat magnum <u>flumen</u>. pueri saepe
3 ex urbe ibant, quod prope <u>flumen</u> ambulare volebant; in <u>flumine</u>
4 multae <u>naves</u> <u>navigabant</u>, quae <u>frumentum</u> ad urbem, <u>vinum</u> ex urbe
5 portabant. pueri has <u>naves</u> laete spectabant, quod saepe <u>nautae</u> eis
6 parva dona <u>iaciebant</u>. olim ubi amici in <u>ripa</u> stabant, <u>naves</u> spectantes,
7 una <u>navis</u> subito ad eos <u>navigavit</u>. simulac <u>navis</u> <u>ripae</u> appropinquavit,
8 duo homines ingentes in <u>ripam</u> <u>desiluerunt</u> et pueros in <u>navem</u>
9 traxerunt. quamquam pueri fortiter <u>resistebant</u>, homines eos facile
10 superaverunt. mox pueri in <u>vinculis</u> erant; homines crudeliores
11 numquam viderant. Sextus iratus clamavit: 'quid vos vultis? cur nos
12 cepistis? nos statim liberate.'
13   unus ex <u>nautis</u> respondit: 'nos sumus <u>piratae</u>. vos iam servi estis. in
14 Gallia cives nobis multam pecuniam semper dant, ubi eis servos
15 <u>vendimus</u>. quod vos estis pueri fortes, maximum <u>pretium</u> accipere
16 possumus. nunc tacete.'
17   pueri, postquam haec <u>verba</u> audiverunt, perterriti erant. ubi
18 <u>circumspectaverunt</u>, decem pueros et paucas puellas prope sedentes
19 conspexerunt. illi quoque in <u>vinculis</u> erant, omnesque timebant.
20   Marcus <u>canem</u> habebat; <u>nomen</u> <u>canis</u> erat Fidus. Fidus semper
21 cum domino ibat. ubi homines dominum amicumque eius capiebant,
22 <u>canis</u> <u>latrabat</u> hominesque <u>oppugnabat</u>; homines tamen eum crudeliter
23 <u>abegerunt</u>. Fidus ad domum celeriter rediit. simulac domum intravit,
24 <u>latravit</u>. Crispus erat pater Marci. Crispus, postquam Fidum audivit,
25 eum tacere <u>iussit</u>. Fidus tamen non tacebat. ubi Crispus Fido
26 appropinquavit, <u>canis</u> ad ianuam cucurrit, deinde sedebat, Crispum
27 spectans. ubi Crispus ad ianuam venit, Fidus in viam cucurrit. <u>ita</u> Fidus
28 Crispum ad <u>flumen</u> duxit.

Names

Sextus, -i m.	Sextus	*Marcus, -i* m.	Marcus
Gallia, -ae f.	Gaul (France)	*Fidus, -i* m.	Fidus
Crispus, -i m.	Crispus		

Words

proximus, -a, -um	neighbouring	*navigo, -are*	I sail
extra + acc.	outside	*frumentum, -i* n.	corn
flumen, -inis n.	river	*vinum, -i* n.	wine
navis, -is f.	ship	*nauta, -ae* m.	sailor

iacio, -ere	I throw	*circumspecto, -are, -avi*	I look round
ripa, -ae f.	river bank	*canis, -is* m.	dog
desilio, -ire, desilui	I jump down	*nomen, -inis* n.	name
resisto, -ere	I resist	*latro, -are*	I bark
vinculum, -i n.	chain	*oppugno, -are*	I attack
pirata, -ae m.	pirate	*abigo, -ere, abegi*	I drive away
vendo, -ere	I sell	*iubeo, -ere, iussi*	I order
pretium, -i n.	price	*ita*	in this way
verbum, -i n.	word		

1   *Sextus ... habitabant* (line 1): what two things are we told about Sextus and Marcus? [3]

2   *extra ... flumen* (line 2): what exactly was outside the city? [1]

3   *pueri saepe ... portabant* (lines 2-5): which **four** of the following statements are true? Write down the letters for the ones that are correct.
      A   the boys left the city occasionally
      B   the boys often left the city
      C   they wanted to swim in the river
      D   they wanted to walk by the river
      E   there were many ships on the river
      F   ships were sailing on many rivers
      G   the ships exported corn and imported wine
      H   the ships exported wine and imported corn [4]

4   *pueri ... iaciebant* (lines 5-6):
      (i)   what did the boys do? [3]
      (ii)   why did they do it? [4]

5   *olim ... navigavit* (lines 6-7): which **three** of the following statements are true? Write down the letters for the ones that are correct.
      A   the boys were standing on the bank
      B   the boys were standing on the ships
      C   the sailors were watching the boys
      D   the boys were watching the ships
      E   one ship suddenly sailed towards the boys
      F   the boys suddenly jumped onto one ship [3]

6   *simulac ... traxerunt* (lines 7-9): what happened as soon as the ship approached the bank? [7]

7   *quamquam ... superaverunt* (lines 9-10):
    (i)   write down and translate the Latin word which describes how
          the boys resisted.   [2]

    (ii) which of the following is the correct translation of *homines eos
          facile superaverunt?*
          A   those men were easily superb
          B   the men easily defeated them
          C   they easily defeated the men
          D   they easily defeated those men   [1]

8   Translate *mox ... viderant* (lines 10-11).   [8]

9   *Sextus ... liberate* (lines 11-12):
    (i)   what **two** questions did Sextus ask?   [4]
    (ii) what did he tell the men to do?   [2]

10 *unus ex nautis respondit* (line 13): which do you think is the best
    translation of these words?
          A   one from the sailors replied
          B   one out of the sailors replied
          C   one of the sailors replied
          D   one ex-sailor replied   [1]

11 *nos sumus piratae. vos iam servi estis* (line 13): write down one word
    from the second of these sentences which contrasts directly with **each**
    of the ones from the first sentence given below:
          A   *nos*
          B   *sumus*
          C   *piratae*   [3]

12 *in Gallia ... vendimus* (lines 13-15): what happened in Gaul? Give full
    details.   [7]

13 *quod ... possumus* (lines 15-16): explain in detail how the pirates would
    gain from having captured the boys.   [6]

14 Which of the following is the correct translation of *nunc tacete* (line 16)?
          A   now be quiet
          B   now you are quiet
          C   now you will be quiet
          D   now we shall be quiet   [1]

15 *pueri ... erant* (line 17): write down and translate the Latin word that
    describes the *pueri*.   [2]

16 Translate *ubi ... conspexerunt* (lines 17-19). [9]

17 *illi ... timebant* (line 19): what **two** things are we told about the other young people? [4]

18 *Marcus ... ibat* (lines 20-21):
   (i)   who or what was Fidus? [1]
   (ii) what did Fidus always do? [2]

19 Translate *ubi ... oppugnabat* (lines 21-22). [10]

20 *homines ... abegerunt* (lines 22-23): what did the men do? [2]

21 *Fidus ... Marci* (lines 23-24): which **three** of the following statements are true? Write down the letters for the ones that are correct.
   A   Fidus slowly went back home
   B   Fidus quickly went back home
   C   Fidus entered and then barked
   D   Fidus barked and then entered
   E   Crispus was the father of Marcus
   F   Crispus went to the father of Marcus [3]

22 *Crispus, postquam ... iussit* (lines 24-25): what did Crispus order Fidus to do? [1]

23 Write down the Latin words from line 25 that tell us that Fidus did not obey Crispus. [1]

24 *ubi Crispus Fido appropinquavit ... duxit* (lines 25-28): explain how Fidus led Crispus to the river. [5]

Total [100]

4b   *After their capture by pirates, Marcus and Sextus are rescued by Crispus and his friend.*

1   Sextus et Marcus erant pueri. hi pueri e domibus discesserant et ad
2   flumen prope urbem iverant. iam perterriti erant, nam piratae eos
3   ceperant. in nave piratarum erant, quae eos ad Galliam portabat.
4   Fidus, qui erat canis fortis et fidelis Marci, Crispum ad flumen duxerat.
5   ille iam in ripa fluminis stabat. Crispus, quamquam iratus erat quod
6   Fidus eum e domo duxerat, circumspectavit. bullam Marci in terra
7   iacentem conspexit. Crispus statim clamavit: 'Marce, Sexte, ubi estis?
8   num in flumen cecidistis?' mortes puerorum timebat.
9   piscator, qui in altera ripa stabat, simulac vocem Crispi audivit,
10 clamavit: 'pueros vidi. duo homines eos in navem traxerunt. navis ad
11 mare ibat.'
12   Crispus rem intellexit, nam piratae multos cives per multos annos
13 abduxerant. ad amicum festinavit, qui navem magnam et celerem
14 habebat. ubi Crispus ad navem advenit, amicus navigare parabat;
15 multi nautae in nave laborabant. postquam Crispus narravit id quod
16 acciderat, amicus nautas navem solvere iussit. navis celeriter ad mare
17 processit. postquam e flumine exierunt, subito alteram navem
18 conspexerunt, quae celeriter fugiebat. navis tamen Crispi et amici
19 celerior erat quam altera. mox ei appropinquaverunt. ubi Crispus
20 'Marce, Sexte, estisne in illa nave?' clamavit, pueri, quamquam
21 Crispum videre non poterant, statim responderunt. piratae gladios
22 strinxerunt et pugnare paraverunt; mox tamen nautae, qui navem
23 Crispi dirigebant, piratas superaverunt. Sextus et Marcus et ceteri
24 captivi laetissimi erant, quod Crispus et amicus eos liberaverant. pueri
25 numquam iterum prope flumen soli ambulabant. cives Crispo et amico,
26 quod tot pueros puellasque liberaverant, magnum praemium dederunt.

Names

Sextus, -i m.	Sextus	*Marcus, -i* m.	Marcus
Gallia, -ae f.	Gaul (France)	*Fidus, -i* m.	Fidus
Crispus, -i m.	Crispus		

Words

flumen, -inis n.	river	*fidelis, -is, -e*	faithful
pirata, -ae m.	pirate	*ripa, -ae* f.	river bank
navis, -is f.	ship	*circumspecto,-are, -avi*	I look round
canis, -is m.	dog	*bulla, -ae* f.	lucky charm

iaceo, -ere	I lie	*iubeo, -ere, iussi*	I order
cado, -ere, cecidi	I fall	*procedo, -ere, -cessi*	I proceed
piscator, -oris m.	fisherman	*gladius, -i* m.	sword
alter, -era, -erum	the other	*stringo, -ere, strinxi*	I draw
mare, -is n.	sea	*dirigo, -ere*	I sail
res, -ei f.	thing, matter	*ceteri, -ae, -a*	the rest of
annus, -i m.	year	*captivus, -i* m.	prisoner
abduco, -ere, -duxi	I kidnap	*iterum*	again
navigo, -are	I sail	*tot*	so many
nauta, -ae m.	sailor	*praemium, -i* n.	reward
navem solvo, -ere	I set sail		

1   *Sextus ... pueri* (line 1): how are Sextus and Marcus described?   [1]

2   *hi pueri ... iverant* (lines 1-2): what **two** things had the *pueri* done?   [5]

3   Write down and translate the Latin word in line 2 that describes Sextus and Marcus.   [2]

4   *nam ... portabat* (lines 2-3): which **three** of the following statements are true? Write down the letters for the ones that are correct.
    A   the boys had captured the pirates
    B   the pirates had captured the boys
    C   the boys were in the pirate ship
    D   the pirates were on ships
    E   the ship had carried the boys to Gaul
    F   the ship was carrying the boys to Gaul   [3]

5   *Fidus ... duxerat* (line 4): what **three** things are we told about Fidus (Marcus' dog)?   [4]

6   *ille ... stabat* (line 5): what was the dog doing?   [2]

7   Translate *Crispus ... circumspectavit* (lines 5-6).   [10]

8   *bullam ... conspexit* (lines 6-7): what made Crispus shout out?   [2]

9   *mortes ... timebat* (line 8): what did Crispus fear?   [2]

10 *piscator ... ibat* (lines 9-11): which **five** of the following statements are true? Write down the letters for the ones that are correct.
    A the fisherman was standing upstream
    B the fisherman was standing across the river
    C the fisherman heard the voice of Crispus
    D Crispus heard the voice of the fisherman
    E the fisherman shouted he had seen the boys
    F Crispus shouted to the fisherman, 'Have you seen the boys?
    G the boys took two men on to the ship
    H two men took the boys on to the ship
    I the ship had gone out to sea
    J the ship was going out to sea   [5]

11 *Crispus rem intellexit* (line 12): which of the following is the best translation of these words?
    A Crispus learned the thing
    B Crispus knew the thing
    C Crispus understood the thing
    D Crispus understood what had happened   [1]

12 *nam ... abduxerant* (lines 12-13): what had the pirates done?   [3]

13 Translate *ad amicum ... habebat* (lines 13-14).   [7]

14 *ubi ... laborabant* (lines 14-15):
    (i)   where was Crispus' friend?   [1]
    (ii) what was he doing?   [1]
    (iii) what else was happening?   [3]

15 *postquam ... iussit* (lines 15-16):
    (i)   what did Crispus do?   [3]
    (ii) what did his friend do?   [2]

16 *navis ... fugiebat* (lines 16-18):
    (i)   did the ship sail up-river or down-river?   [1]
    (ii) what did Crispus and his friend see when they left the river?   [1]
    (iii) what was this doing?   [2]

17 Translate *navis ... altera* (lines 18-19).   [8]

18 Which of the following is the correct translation of *mox ei*
appropinquaverunt (line 19)?
    A soon they approached
    B soon they approached it
    C soon they were approaching it
    D night approached them   [1]

19 *ubi ... responderunt* (lines 19-21): which **four** of the following
statements are true? Write down the letters for the ones that are
correct.
    A Marcus and Sextus called to Crispus
    B Crispus called to Marcus and Sextus
    C 'Are you in that ship?' was the question asked
    D 'Is that the ship?' was the question asked
    E the boys were able to see Crispus
    F the boys were not able to see Crispus
    G the boys were unable to reply
    H the boys replied   [4]

20 *piratae ... paraverunt* (lines 21-22): what **two** things did the pirates
do?   [3]

21 *mox ... superaverunt* (lines 22-23): what was the result of the fight? [3]

22 Translate *Sextus ... liberaverant* (lines 23-24).   [11]

23 *pueri ... ambulabant* (lines 24-25): what did the boys never do
again?   [3]

24 *cives ... dederunt* (lines 25-26):
    (i)   what did the citizens do?   [3]
    (ii) why did they do this?   [3]

                                                    Total [100]

5 *A priest of the goddess Isis trying to protect his city is interrupted by a Christian.*

1 Octavius erat <u>sacerdos</u>. Octavius in <u>templo</u> Isidis habitabat. multi cives
2 Isidem <u>colebant</u>, quod dea aliam <u>vitam</u> <u>post</u> mortem <u>promittebat</u>.
3 Octavius iam laetus erat, quod <u>ver</u> advenerat.
4   Octavius <u>pompam</u> per mediam urbem ducebat. cives omnes in viis
5 stabant, <u>statuam</u> deae exspectantes. Octavius et quinque alii
6 <u>sacerdotes</u> <u>statuam</u> in <u>umeris</u> portabant. cives <u>flores</u> ad <u>pedes</u>
7 <u>sacerdotum</u> <u>iaciebant</u>.
8   <u>pompa</u> ad <u>forum</u> lente iter fecit. <u>sacerdotes</u>, simulatque in medium
9 <u>forum</u> venerunt, <u>statuam</u> in terra posuerunt. tum <u>principes</u> <u>statuae</u>
10 appropinquaverunt, dona portantes. <u>favorem</u> deae petebant. 'da nobis
11 bonam <u>fortunam</u> ac <u>frumentum</u> plurimum,' rogaverunt <u>principes</u>.
12 Octavius, quod erat <u>dux</u> <u>sacerdotum</u>, <u>pro</u> dea respondit. 'dea,' inquit,
13 'hanc urbem semper <u>curat</u>, quod cives sunt <u>pii</u>. dea civibus optimam
14 <u>fortunam</u> dare vult.'
15   omnes cives erant laetissimi. sed erat unus vir, Petrus, qui iratus
16 erat. Petrus erat Christianus, et alios deos videre nolebat; Christo soli
17 credebat. subito Petrus inter <u>principes</u> cucurrit. 'Isis non est dea,'
18 clamavit. 'Christus solus vos <u>servare</u> potest. Christum, non Isidem,
19 <u>colite</u>.' <u>principes</u>, ubi haec <u>verba</u> audiverunt, 'discede,' clamaverunt. 'tu
20 nihil intellegis. Isis est optima dea. Isis nobis semper <u>favet</u>. de <u>tuo</u> deo
21 audire nolumus.' tum Petrus, 'in <u>nomine</u> Christi,' respondit, 'vobis
22 omnibus <u>maledico</u>. Christus vos <u>punire</u> debet.' <u>principes</u>, postquam
23 haec audiverunt, hominem <u>rapuerunt</u> et in <u>carcerem</u> eum traxerunt.
24   <u>post</u> paucos <u>dies</u>, erat magna <u>tempestas</u>, quae <u>agros</u> et domos
25 <u>delevit</u>, multosque cives necavit. Petrus, simulatque hoc <u>cognovit</u>, risit.
26 'meus deus,' inquit, 'vos <u>punivit</u>, <u>sicut</u> dixi.' <u>principes</u> irati responderunt:
27 'deus <u>tuus</u>, <u>si</u> hoc fecit, crudelissimus est. nemo deum tam crudelem
28 <u>colere</u> vult. <u>culpa</u> est <u>tua</u>. te <u>punire</u> debemus.' itaque <u>principes</u>
29 <u>carnificibus</u> virum tradiderunt.

Names

Octavius, -i m.	Octavius	*Isis, -idis* f.	Isis (a goddess)
Petrus, -i m.	Peter	*Christianus, -i*	Christian
Christus, -i m.	Christ		

Words

sacerdos, -otis m.	priest	*post* + acc.	after
templum, -i n.	temple	*promitto, -ere*	I promise
colo, -ere	I worship	*ver, veris* n.	spring
vita, -ae f.	life	*pompa, -ae* f.	procession

statua, -ae f.	statue	*faveo, -ere* + dat.	I favour
umerus, -i m.	shoulder	*tuus, -a, -um*	your
flos, floris m.	flower	*nomen, -inis* n.	name
pes, pedis m.	foot	*maledico, -ere* + dat.	I curse
iacio, -ere	I throw	*punio, -ire*	I punish
forum, -i n.	forum, market-	*rapio, -ere, -ui*	I seize
	place	*carcer, -eris* m.	prison
princeps, -ipis m.	leader	*dies, -ei* m.	day
favor, -oris m.	favour	*tempestas, -atis* f.	storm
fortuna, -ae f.	fortune	*ager, -ri* m.	field
frumentum, -i n.	corn	*deleo, -ere, -evi*	I destroy
dux, ducis m.	leader	*cognosco, -ere, -novi*	I learn
pro + abl.	on behalf of	*sicut*	just as
curo, -are	I look after	*si*	if
pius, -a, -um	respectful	*culpa, -ae* f.	blame
servo, -are	I protect	*carnifex, -icis* m.	executioner
verbum, -i n.	word		

1   What do we learn about Octavius in line 1?   [2]

2   *multi ... promittebat* (lines 1-2):
    (i)   how popular was the worship of Isis?   [1]
    (ii)   why was this?   [3]

3   Translate *Octavius ... advenerat* (line 3).   [6]

4   *Octavius ... ducebat* (line 4): what was Octavius doing?   [3]

5   *cives ... exspectantes* (lines 4-5): which **two** of the following statements are true? Write down the letters for the correct ones.
    A   all the citizens were standing in the streets
    B   citizens were standing in all the streets
    C   the goddess was waiting for her statue
    D   the citizens were waiting for the statue of the goddess   [2]

6   *Octavius ... portabant* (lines 5-6): how many people carried the statue?   [1]

7   *cives ... iaciebant* (lines 6-7): what were the citizens doing?   [2]

8   *pompa ... fecit* (line 8): what are we told here about the procession? [3]

9   Translate *sacerdotes ... posuerunt* (lines 8-9).   [7]

10 *tum ... petebant* (lines 9-10):
    (i)   what **two** things did the leaders do? [4]
    (ii)   what was their reason for doing these things? [2]

11 *da ... principes* (lines 10-11):
    (i)   which is the correct translation of *da nobis*?
        A give us
        B we give
        C she gives us
        D the nobleman gave [1]
    (ii)   what **two** things did the leaders want? [2]

12 *Octavius ... respondit* (line 12):
    (i)   what did Octavius do? [2]
    (ii)   why did he do this? [1]

13 *dea ... vult* (lines 12-14): which **four** of the following statements are true? Write down the letters for the correct ones.
        A the goddess spoke
        B Octavius spoke
        C the goddess looks after the city
        D the city looks after the goddess
        E the citizens are respectful to the goddess
        F the goddess is respectful to the citizens
        G the citizens want good fortune for the goddess
        H the goddess wants good fortune for the citizens [4]

14 Translate *omnes cives erant laetissimi* (line 15). [5]

15 *sed ... nolebat* (lines 15-16):
    (i)   how did Peter feel? [1]
    (ii)   what **two** reasons are given for this? [5]

16 Which is the best translation of *Christo soli credebat* (lines 16-17)?
        A he believed Christ alone
        B he trusted only to Christ
        C he gave his trust only to Christ
        D he believed only in Christ [1]

17 Translate *subito ... cucurrit* (line 17). [4]

18 *Isis ... potest* (lines 17-18):
    (i)   what did Peter say about Isis? [2]
    (ii)   what did he say about Christ? [3]

19 *Christum ... colite* (lines 18-19): what command did Peter give?　　[2]

20 *principes ... intellegis* (lines 19-20): which **three** of the following
 statements are true? Write down the letters for the correct ones.
　　A　the leaders heard Peter's words
　　B　Peter heard the leaders' words
　　C　the leaders told Peter to leave
　　D　the leaders shouted as they left
　　E　the leaders said Peter was not intelligent
　　F　the leaders said Peter understood nothing　　[3]

21 Write down and translate the Latin word that describes the goddess
 Isis in line 20.　　[2]

22 Which is the correct translation of *Isis nobis semper favet* (line 20)?
　　A　our Isis is always favourable
　　B　we always favour Isis
　　C　Isis always favours us
　　D　Isis always favours the nobility　　[1]

23 Translate *de tuo deo audire nolumus* (lines 20-21).　　[4]

24 *tum ... debet* (lines 21-22): how did Peter reply to the leaders?　Make
 two points.　　[4]

25 *principes ... traxerunt* (lines 22-23): what happened to Peter?　　[2]

26 *post ... necavit* (lines 24-25):
　　(i)　what natural event occurred?　　[1]
　　(ii)　when did this occur?　　[1]
　　(iii)　what were the **three** results of this event?　　[4]

27 Write down and translate the Latin word that tells us how Peter
 reacted to the event (line 25).　　[2]

28 *meus ... dixi* (line 26): how did Peter explain the event?　　[2]

29 *si ... est* (line 27):
　　(i)　name *tuus deus*.　　[1]
　　(ii)　how did the leaders describe *tuus deus*?　　[1]
　　(iii)　why did they describe him like this?　　[1]

30 Which is the correct translation of *nemo ... vult* (lines 27-28)?
   A no one wants to worship such a cruel god
   B no god so cruel wants to be worshipped
   C such a cruel god wants no one to worship him
   D no one so cruel wants to worship a god   [1]

31 What happened to Peter at the end?   [1]

Total [100]

6   *A slave-girl objects to the way she is treated.*

1   Labrax erat venalicius. Labrax servos in multis urbibus vendebat.
2   primum servos in Gallia emebat, deinde eos in nave ad Italiam
3   transportabat. Romani, quod semper servos emere volebant, multam
4   pecuniam dare parati erant. itaque Labrax iam divitissimus erat. optimi
5   servi erant ei qui legere poterant. Labrax laetus quoque erat, ubi
6   ancillam pulchram vendebat.
7   inter ancillas quas Labrax vendebat erat Aoife. Aoife fuerat femina
8   nobilis, quae in Gallia habitaverat. milites Romani, postquam urbem
9   Aoifes superaverunt, omnes feminas puellasque ceperant; deinde
10 venaliciis eas vendiderant. Labrax, quod multam pecuniam habebat,
11 feminas puellasque optimas emere potuerat.
12   iam Aoife in foro Romae stabat, novum dominum exspectans. vir qui
13 eam emit erat Lepidus. Lepidus multos servos iam habebat; sed inter
14 ancillas eius nulla erat pulchrior quam Aoife. Lepidus laetus erat, quod
15 Aoife intellegebat omnia quae dicebat. Lepidus ei epistulam tradidit;
16 Aoife verba facile recitavit. Lepidus amicos ad cenam invitaverat.
17 simulatque omnes accubuerunt, Aoife triclinium intravit, cibum portans.
18 omnes, ubi eam viderunt, attoniti erant, Lepidumque laudaverunt.
19 postquam cenaverunt, Aoife versus recitavit. unus ex amicis Lepidi,
20 'huc veni, carissima,' inquit. 'tibi osculum dare volo.' Aoife, quae erat
21 irata, ei non paruit. homo iratissimus dixit: 'tu nunc eam punire debes,
22 Lepide.' Lepidus respondit, 'ita vero, sed cras id facere possum. iam
23 bibe. Aoife, amicis plus vini da.'
24   postridie Lepidus Aoifem arcessivit. illa ad eum festinavit. 'cur heri tu
25 amico parere noluisti?' eam iratus rogavit. 'quod ego femina nobilis
26 sum,' Aoife respondit. 'sed tu ancilla es,' Lepidus dixit. 'in domo tua
27 sum ancilla,' Aoife respondit. 'in corde meo tamen sum filia regis. ego
28 tibi animam tradere nolo.' Lepidus attonitus eam non punivit.

34

Names

Labrax, -acis m.	Labrax	Gallia, -ae f.	Gaul (France)
Italia, -ae f.	Italy	Romani, -orum m.pl.	the Romans
Aoife, -es f.	Aoife	Romanus, -a, -um	Roman
Lepidus, -i m.	Lepidus	Roma, -ae f.	Rome

Words

venalicius, -i m.	slave dealer	ceno, -are, -avi	I dine
vendo, -ere, -didi	I sell	versus, -us m.	poem
emo, -ere, emi	I buy	huc	over here
navis, -is f.	ship	carus, -a, -um	dear
transporto, -are	I transport	osculum, -i n.	kiss
paratus, -a, -um	ready	pareo, -ere, -ui + dat.	I obey
dives, -itis	rich	punio, -ire, -ivi	I punish
nobilis, -is, -e	noble	ita vero	yes
forum, -i n.	forum, market-place	cras	tomorrow
		bibo, -ere	I drink
verbum, -i n.	word	vinum, -i n.	wine
recito, -are, -avi	I read aloud	postridie	next day
invito, -are, -avi	I invite	arcesso, -ere, -ivi	I summon
accumbo, -ere, -bui	I lie down	cor, cordis n.	heart
triclinium, -i n.	dining room	anima, -ae f.	soul
attonitus, -a, -um	astonished		

1   Labrax ... vendebat: (line 1): where did Labrax sell his slaves?   [2]

2   primum ... transportabat (lines 2-3): which **three** of the following statements are true? Write down the letters for the ones that are correct.
   A   he first bought the slaves in Gaul
   B   he bought the first slaves in Gaul
   C   then he transported them in ships
   D   then he transported them in a ship
   E   the slaves ended up in Italy
   F   he took the slaves out of Italy   [3]

3   Translate Romani ... erant (lines 3-4).   [10]

4   Write down and translate the Latin word in line 4 that describes Labrax.   [2]

35

5 *optimi ... vendebat* (lines 4-6):
   (i)   which were the best slaves? [2]
   (ii) how do you think Labrax felt when he had such slaves? [1]
   (iii) what else made him feel this way? [3]

6 *inter ... Aoife* (line 7): what are we told about Aoife here? [3]

7 Translate *Aoife ... habitaverat* (lines 7-8). [6]

8 *milites ... vendiderant* (lines 8-10): which **three** of the following statements are true? Write down the letters for the ones that are correct.
    A Roman soldiers overpowered Aoife behind the city
    B Roman soldiers overpowered Aoife's city
    C the soldiers had captured all the women and girls
    D the soldiers had all captured women and girls
    E the soldiers had sold the women and girls to slave dealers
    F slave dealers had sold them to the soldiers [3]

9 *Labrax ... potuerat* (lines 10-11):
   (i)   what had Labrax been able to do? [4]
   (ii) why was he able to do this? [3]

10 Translate *iam ... exspectans* (line 12). [8]

11 *vir ... Lepidus* (lines 12-13): what did Lepidus do? [1]

12 Which is the correct translation of *Lepidus multos servos iam habebat* (line 13)?
    A now Lepidus lived with many slaves
    B already Lepidus had had many slaves
    C Lepidus already had many slaves
    D many slaves now live with Lepidus [1]

13 Translate *sed ... Aoife* (lines13-14). [9]

14 *Lepidus ... dicebat* (lines 14-15): what made Lepidus happy? [4]

15 *Lepidus ... recitavit* (lines 15-16):
   (i)   why do you think Lepidus handed Aoife a letter? [1]
   (ii) what did Aoife do? [2]

16 *Lepidus ... invitaverat* (line 16): what had Lepidus done? [2]

17 *Aoife ... portans* (line 17): what was Aoife's job here? [2]

18 *omnes ... laudaverunt* (line 18):
   (i)   why do you think everyone was astonished? [1]
   (ii) why do you think they praised Lepidus rather than Aoife? [1]

19 *postquam ... recitavit* (line 19): what was Aoife's second task? [1]

20 *unus ... volo* (lines 19-20):
   (i)   who gave an order here? [2]
   (ii) to whom did he give the order? [1]
   (iii) what was the order? [1]
   (iv) what did he say he wanted to do? [1]

21 *Aoife ... dixit* (lines 20-21): what contrast is made here between
Aoife and the man? [2]

22 *homo ... possum* (lines 21-22):
   (i)   what did the man say to Lepidus? [3]
   (ii) what did Lepidus prefer to do? [2]

23 *Aoife ... da* (line 23): which is the correct translation of these words?
       A Aoife gave the friends more wine
       B Aoife, give the friends more wine
       C Aoife gave wine to more of the friends
       D Aoife, give wine to more of the friends [1]

24 *postridie ... festinavit* (line 24): what did Aoife do when summoned? [2]

25 *cur ... rogavit* (lines 24-25): what did Lepidus ask Aoife? [4]

26 *quod ... dixit* (lines 25-26): what different views of Aoife's situation did
she and Lepidus have? [2]

27 *in domo ... nolo* (lines 26-28): in your own words, explain Aoife's
argument. [3]

28 *Lepidus ... punivit* (line 28): why do you think Lepidus did not punish
her? [1]

Total [100]

7a *Livia goes to her country house to escape the heat of the city.*

1 Severus erat mercator. Severus magnam domum in urbe habebat. in
2 hac domo Severus cum uxore habitabat. Severus tamen, quod erat
3 dives, villam quoque habebat. haec villa erat pulcherrima etiamque
4 maior quam domus. villa in mediis montibus stabat. Severus ad villam
5 non saepe ibat, quod semper in urbe laborabat.
6 　　　Livia erat uxor Severi. Livia villam amabat, quod in montibus aer
7 semper iucundior erat quam in urbe. sed ibi sola manere nolebat.
8 Severus, quod villam raro visitabat, vilicum habebat. vilicus erat Sparax.
9 Sparax, quamquam erat servus, multos alios servos in villa curabat. hi
10 servi villam purgabant et in agris laborabant.
11 　　　Livia aestum in urbe diutius ferre non poterat. Livia, simulac maritus
12 ad domum rediit, 'volo,' inquit, 'ad villam nostram ire. hic in urbe nimis
13 calidum est. visne mecum ad villam ire?' 'id facere non possum,'
14 Severus respondit. 'cras plurimum frumentum ad portum ferre debeo.
15 deinde tres naves vinum portantes exspecto.' uxor dixit: 'quamquam ad
16 villam sola ire nolo, hic manere non possum. tu postea veni.'
17 　　　Livia cum duobus servis celeriter discessit. post tres dies ad villam
18 advenerunt. ubi Sparax eos conspexit, attonitus erat, quod nullus
19 servus ei epistulam antea tulerat; laetus quoque erat Liviam videre,
20 quod dominam clam amabat. Sparax, quamquam servus erat, semper
21 cenam in triclinio consumebat; alii servi ei cibum portabant. nunc
22 difficile ei erat id facere, quod servi cum dominis cenare numquam
23 debebant. Livia tamen, quod erat femina benigna, nolebat eum in culina
24 cum ceteris servis cenare iubere; nolebat quoque sola cenare. itaque
25 Livia et Sparax una cenaverunt.

Names

Severus, -i m.	Severus	Livia, -ae f.	Livia
Sparax, -acis m.	Sparax		

Words

mercator, -oris m.	merchant	purgo, -are	I clean
dives, -itis	rich	ager, -ri m.	field
villa, -ae f.	country house	aestus, -us m.	heat
mons, -tis m.	mountain	diutius	any longer
aer, -is m.	air	fero, ferre, tuli	I put up with
iucundus, -a, -um	pleasant	hic	here
raro	rarely	nimis	too
visito, -are	I visit	calidus, -a, -um	hot
vilicus, -i m.	manager	cras	tomorrow
curo, -are	I supervise	frumentum, -i n.	corn

portus, -us m.	harbour	*triclinium, -i* n.	dining room
navis, -is f.	ship	*ceno, -are*	I dine
vinum, -i n.	wine	*benignus, -a, -um*	kindly
postea	later	*culina, -ae* f.	kitchen
dies, -ei m.	day	*ceteri, -ae, -a*	the rest of
antea	beforehand	*iubeo, -ere*	I order
clam	secretly	*una*	together

1 *Severus ... habebat* (line 1): give **two** details of Severus' house.　[2]

2 *in hac domo ... habitabat* (lines 1- 2): with whom did Severus share the house?　[1]

3 *Severus ... habebat* (lines 2-3):
(i) what other possession did Severus have?　[1]
(ii) why was he able to have this possession?　[1]

4 *haec ... domus* (lines 3-4): which **two** of the following statements are true? Write down the letters for the correct ones.
A the country house was beautiful
B the country house was very beautiful
C the country house was even larger than the town house
D the town house was even larger than the country house　[2]

5 *villa ... stabat* (line 4): where was the country house situated?　[2]

6 Translate *Severus ... laborabat* (lines 4-5).　[9]

7 *Livia erat uxor Severi* (line 6): who was Livia?　[2]

8 *Livia villam ... urbe* (lines 6-7): explain fully why Livia loved the country house.　[6]

9 Translate *sed ibi sola manere nolebat* (line 7).　[5]

10 *Severus ... habebat* (line 8): why did Severus need to have a manager?　[2]

11 Which is the correct translation of *quamquam erat servus* (line 9)?
A who was a slave
B when he was a slave
C although he was a slave
D the slave was somewhere　[1]

12 *multos ... curabat* (line 9): what was the manager's job?　[4]

13 *hi … laborabant* (lines 9-10): what jobs did the other slaves do? [2]

14 *Livia … poterat* (line 11): what could Livia not do? [3]

15 Translate *Livia, simulac … ire* (lines 11-12). [10]

16 Which is the correct translation of *visne mecum ad villam ire* (line 13)?
    A do you want me to go to the house?
    B will you go with me to the house?
    C do you want to come to me at the house?
    D do you want to go with me to the house? [1]

17 *id facere … exspecto* (lines 13-15): which **four** of the following
statements are true? Write down the letters for the correct ones.
    A Severus was not able to do what Livia asked
    B Severus was able to do what Livia asked
    C the next day Severus was to take delivery of a lot of corn
    D the next day Severus was to take a lot of corn to the harbour
    E three ships were waiting for Severus
    F Severus was expecting three ships
    G the ships were carrying wine
    H Severus was to carry wine to put on the ships [4]

18 *uxor … veni* (lines 15-16):
    (i)   what did Livia not want to do? [3]
    (ii)   what was she unable to do? [1]
    (iii) what did she tell Severus to do? [2]

19 Translate *Livia … discessit* (line 17). [6]

20 *post … advenerunt* (lines 17-18): how long was the journey? [2]

21 *ubi … tulerat* (lines 18-19):
    (i)   why was Sparax astonished when he caught sight of Livia? [5]
    (ii) what do you think the letter might have said? [1]

22 *laetus … amabat* (lines 19-20): why did Sparax feel happy to see
Livia? [2]

23 *Sparax … portabant* (lines 20-21):
    (i)   what did Sparax always do? [2]
    (ii) what was surprising about this? [1]
    (iii) what did other slaves do for Sparax? [3]

24 *nunc ... debebant* (lines 21-23): which **two** of the following statements
   are true? Write down the letters for the correct ones.
   A it was difficult for Sparax to dine as he had done
   B Sparax found dining difficult
   C slaves should never dine with their owners
   D slaves and their owners should never dine   [2]

25 *Livia ... iubere* (lines 23-24):
   (i)   write down the Latin adjective that tells us what sort of person
         Livia was.   [1]
   (ii) what was the result of her being this sort of person?   [6]

26 *nolebat quoque ... cenaverunt* (lines 24-25):
   (i)   what did Livia not want to do?   [1]
   (ii) what happened as a result of this?   [3]
   (iii) do you think Livia was wise or foolish to allow this to happen?
         Give a reason for your answer.   [1]

Total [100]

7b *Severus pays a surprise visit to the country house.*

1 Sparax erat vilicus. Sparax in villa Severi habitabat et laborabat.
2 domina Sparacis, Livia, ad villam venerat. heri Livia cum Sparace
3 cenaverat. postridie Sparax, 'dic mihi, domina,' inquit: 'nonne iam
4 libertus sum?' 'cur hoc rogas?' dixit Livia. 'quod heri me ad cenam
5 invitavisti. secundum legem, me liberavisti,' Sparax respondit. Livia
6 attonita atque irata erat, et maritum timebat. tandem dixit: 'noli hoc
7 marito meo nuntiare. nonne villam curare vis?' 'ita vero, Livia,' Sparax
8 respondit. 'sed mihi pecuniam dare iam debes.' Livia invita consensit.

9   Sparax vir intellegens et doctus erat. ubi Livia eum de vita priore
10 rogavit, ille respondit: 'ego eram princeps in Britannia. postquam
11 Romani civitatem meam ceperunt, me et paucos alios vendiderunt.
12 maritus tuus me emit. Severus, quod ego solitus eram homines ducere,
13 mihi hunc laborem dedit. vita satis iucunda erat.'

14   saepe, ubi Sparax servos inspiciebat, Livia cum eo ambulabat. saepe
15 cum eo ad proximam urbem iter faciebat. mox similes uxori et marito
16 erant, quod omnia una faciebant.

17   ubi ad villam ex urbe olim redierunt, attoniti Severum eos
18 exspectantem conspexerunt. ille laborem confecerat, et iam uxorem
19 iterum videre volebat. ubi uxorem exspectabat, alios servos
20 interrogaverat. iratissimus fuerat, simulac de amicitia uxoris et Sparacis
21 cognovit. 'cur,' uxori clamavit, 'tu Sparacem inter amicos nunc habes?
22 ille est servus.' 'eheu!' respondit uxor. 'Sparax nunc libertus est.' 'quid?'
23 rogavit Severus, etiam iratior. 'eum ad cenam invitavi,' inquit Livia. 'cur
24 id fecisti? num stulta es?' Severus rogavit. 'id feci,' respondit Livia,
25 'quod Sparacem amo. te non iam amo. quod tu semper laboras, ego te
26 numquam video.' Severus tristissimus erat, nam laboraverat quod
27 volebat uxorem satis pecuniae habere. sed quid facere potuit?

Names

Sparax, -acis m.	Sparax	*Livia, -ae* f.	Livia
Britannia, -ae f.	Britain	*Romani, -orum* m.pl.	the Romans
Severus, -i m.	Severus		

Words

vilicus, -i m.	manager	*attonitus, -a, -um*	astonished
villa, -ae f.	country house	*nuntio, -are*	I report
ceno, -are	I have dinner	*curo, -are*	I look after
postridie	on the next day	*ita vero*	yes
libertus, -i m.	freedman	*invitus, -a, -um*	unwilling
invito, -are, -avi	I invite	*consentio, -ire, -sensi*	I agree
secundum legem	according to the law	*intellegens, -ntis*	intelligent
		doctus, -a, -um	clever

vita, -ae f.	life	*proximus, -a, -um*	nearest
prior, -oris	previous	*similis, -is, -e* + dat.	similar
princeps, -ipis m.	chieftain	*una*	together
civitas, -atis f.	town	*conficio, -ere, -feci*	I complete
vendo, -ere, -didi	I sell	*iterum*	again
emo, -ere, emi	I buy	*interrogo, -are, -avi*	I question
solitus, -a, -um	accustomed	*amicitia, -ae* f.	friendship
labor, -oris m.	job	*cognosco, -ere, -novi*	I learn
satis	enough	*eheu!*	oh dear!
iucundus, -a, -um	pleasant	*tristis, -is, -e*	sad
inspicio, -ere	I inspect		

1   *Sparax ... laborabat* (line 1): what **two** things did Sparax do in
Severus' country house?   [2]

2   Which is the correct translation of *domina Sparacis ad villam venerat*
(line 2)?
     A   Sparax's mistress was coming to the country house
     B   Sparax's mistress came to the country house
     C   Sparax's mistress had come to the country house
     D   Sparax's master came to the country house   [1]

3   *heri ... cenaverat* (lines 2-3): what had Livia done the previous day?   [1]

4   *postridie ... sum* (lines 3-4): which **three** of the following statements are
true? Write down the letters for the correct ones.
     A   Sparax spoke to Livia on the next day
     B   Livia spoke to Sparax on the next day
     C   Sparax asked his mistress to answer a question
     D   Sparax said he had asked his mistress a question
     E   the question was 'Surely I am now a freedman?'
     F   the question was 'Surely I am not now a freedman?'   [3]

5   *quod ... invitavisti* (lines 4-5): what did Sparax say Livia had done?   [2]

6   *secundum ... liberavisti* (line 5): how did he think Livia's action
had affected him?   [2]

7   *Livia ... timebat* (lines 5-6): in what **three** ways did Livia react to what
Sparax said to her?   [4]

8   (i)   Translate *noli ... nuntiare* (lines 6-7).   [5]
    (ii)   Why do you think Livia said these words?   [1]

9 *nonne ... vis* (line 7): was Livia expecting the answer 'yes' or 'no'
   to this question?   [1]

10 Translate *sed ... debes* (line 8).   [6]

11 *ubi ... rogavit* (lines 9-10): what did Livia ask Sparax about?   [1]

12 *ille ... vendiderunt* (lines 10-12): which **four** of the following statements
   are true? Write down the letters for the correct ones.
            A Sparax had been a chieftain in Rome
            B Sparax had been a chieftain in Britain
            C Sparax captured the Roman town
            D the Romans captured Sparax' town
            E Sparax sold a few other men
            F the Romans sold Sparax
            G the Romans sold a few other men as well as Sparax
            H others sold Sparax and a few men   [4]

13 *maritus ... erat* (lines 12-13):
   (i)   what **two** things happened to Sparax?   [4]
   (ii)   why did Severus treat Sparax in the way he did?   [4]
   (iii) what job do you think is meant by *hunc laborem*?   [1]
   (iv)   was Sparax satisfied with his life or not?   [1]

14 *saepe ubi ... faciebat* (lines 14-15):
   (i)   what are we told first that Livia often did?   [2]
   (ii)   when did she do this?   [2]
   (iii) what else did Livia do with Sparax?   [3]

15 Translate *mox ... faciebant* (lines 15-16).   [8]

16 *ubi ... conspexerunt* (lines 17-18):
   (i)   when were Livia and Sparax astonished?   [2]
   (ii)   why were they astonished?   [2]

17 *ille ... volebat* (lines 18-19): give **two** reasons why Severus had
   come.   [4]

18 Which is the correct translation of *ubi uxorem exspectabat* (line 19)?
            A when he was waiting for his wife
            B when his wife was waiting for him
            C when his wife was expecting
            D when he had waited for his wife   [1]

19 *alios ... cognovit* (lines 19-21):
    (i)   write down and translate the Latin word describing Severus.   [3]
    (ii)   what had he done that made him feel this way?   [2]
    (iii)   what had Severus found out about?   [2]

20 *cur ... est* (lines 21-22): which **three** of the following statements are true? Write down the letters for the correct ones.
    A Severus shouted to his wife
    B Severus' wife shouted to him
    C one of them asked, 'Why are you friends with Sparax?'
    D one of them asked, 'Why is Sparax living among friends?'
    E one of them said, 'They are slaves.'
    F one of them said, 'Sparax is a slave.'   [3]

21 *'eheu!'* (line 22): why do you think Livia said this?   [1]

22 *Sparax ... est* (line 22): what did Livia tell her husband?   [2]

23 *quid ... iratior* (line 22-23):
    (i)   how did Severus now feel when he heard what Livia said?   [2]
    (ii)   which of the following words do you think best describes Severus when he said *quid*?
        A surprised
        B happy
        C satisfied
        D proud   [1]

24 Translate *cur ... rogavit* (lines 23-24).   [8]

25 *id feci ... video* (lines 24-26):
    (i)   in line 25, what contrast did Livia make between her feelings for Severus and those for Sparax?   [2]
    (ii)   explain what had caused Livia's attitude towards her husband to change.   [4]

26 *Severus ... potuit* (lines 26-27): which **three** of the following statements are true? Write down the letters for the correct ones.
    A Severus was sadder
    B Severus was very sad
    C Severus had worked as his wife wanted enough money
    D Severus had worked to provide his wife with enough money
    E there was nothing Severus could do about it
    F there were several things Severus could do about it   [3]

Total [100]

8   *Helena falls in love with an unsuitable young man.*

1   Helena Iulium amabat. Iulius erat iuvenis pulcher, qui in <u>proxima</u>
2   domo habitabat. pater Helenae erat vir <u>nobilis</u>, sed pater Iulii erat vir
3   <u>pauper</u>. itaque pater Helenae patrem Iulii etiam salutare nolebat.
4   Helena, ubi in via ambulabat, saepe Iulium conspiciebat et salutabat;
5   ille semper laete ridebat. <u>cotidie</u> Iulius cum amicis ad <u>palaestram</u>
6   prope mediam urbem ibat; <u>cotidie</u> Helena prope portam <u>palaestrae</u>
7   stabat, eum exspectans. pater Helenae tamen, simulatque hoc vidit,
8   filiae dixit: 'noli illum iuvenem salutare. tu maritum meliorem quam
9   illum habere debes.'
10 Helena, quamquam id quod pater dixerat facere volebat, <u>amorem</u>
11 <u>relinquere</u> non poterat. <u>postridie</u>, ubi Iulium conspexit, 'ego te amo,'
12 inquit. iuvenis <u>attonitus</u> erat, sed laetus quoque, quod Helenam
13 spectare ei diu <u>placuerat</u>; nam Helena erat pulchrior quam omnes
14 aliae puellae, quae in urbe habitabant. <u>postea</u> Iulius, ubi per vias urbis
15 ambulabat, semper <u>circumspectabat</u>, Helenam quaerens; illa semper
16 <u>aderat</u>. tandem Iulius Helenam amabat <u>tantum quantum</u> illa eum
17 amabat.
18 sed <u>quo modo</u> <u>amorem</u> <u>ostendere</u> poterant? Helena neque Iulium in
19 domum suam <u>invitare</u> poterat, neque in domum eius intrare. non <u>satis</u>
20 erat Helenae Iulium in via videre; iam eum amicum esse volebat. mox
21 Helena <u>desperans</u> cibum consumere nolebat. <u>post</u> paucos <u>dies</u> pater
22 et mater <u>anxii</u>, 'cur,' inquiunt, 'tu <u>tam</u> <u>tristis</u> es, filia? cur cenam non
23 consumis? num mortem <u>cupis</u>?' Helena respondit: 'hoc facio quod
24 Iulium amo, sed vos crudeles me non <u>sinitis</u> eum etiam videre. iam
25 vivere nolo.' Helena e domo fugit lacrimans. pater, quamquam iratus
26 erat, nihil aliud facere potuit quam <u>amorem</u> eorum accipere. duo
27 <u>amantes</u> erant laetissimi.

Names

Helena, -ae f.	Helena	*Iulius, -i* m.	Julius

Words

proximus, -a, -um	next door	*placet, -ere, -uit* + dat.	it pleases
nobilis, -is, -e	noble	*postea*	afterwards
pauper, -eris	poor	*circumspecto, -are*	I look round
cotidie	every day	*adsum, -esse*	I am there
palaestra, -ae f.	sports ground	*tantum quantum*	as much as
amor, -oris m.	love	*quo modo?*	how?
relinquo, -ere	I abandon	*ostendo, -ere*	I show
postridie	next day	*invito, -are*	I invite
attonitus, -a, -um	astonished	*satis*	enough

despero, -are	I despair	*tristis, -is, -e*	sad
post + acc.	after	*cupio, -ere*	I desire
dies, -ei m.	day	*sino, -ere*	I allow
anxius, -a, -um	anxious	*amans, -ntis* m.	lover
tam	so		

1   Which is the correct translation of *Helena Iulium amabat* (line 1)?
    A   Helena loves Julius
    B   Helena loved Julius
    C   Helena had loved Julius
    D   Julius had loved Helena   [1]

2   *Iulius ... habitabat* (lines 1-2): what **two** facts are given here
    about Julius?   [4]

3   *pater ... pauper* (lines 2-3): what contrast is made between the
    two fathers?   [2]

4   Translate *itaque ... nolebat* (line 3).   [8]

5   *Helena ... ridebat* (lines 4-5): which **three** of the following statements
    are true? Write down the letters for the correct ones.
    A   Helena used to walk in the street
    B   Julius didn't walk in the street
    C   Julius used to catch sight of Helena
    D   Helena used to catch sight of Julius
    E   Julius always used to smile
    F   Helena always used to smile   [3]

6   *cotidie Iulius ... exspectans* (lines 5-7):
    (i)   what did Julius do every day? Give full details.   [6]
    (ii)   what **two** things did Helena do every day?   [5]

7   *pater ... salutare* (lines 7-8):
    (i)   when did Helena's father speak to her?   [2]
    (ii)   what did he forbid her to do?   [2]

8   Translate *tu ... debes* (lines 8-9).   [6]

9   *Helena ... poterat* (lines 10-11): explain in your own words Helena's
    feelings about what her father had said to her.   [2]

10 *postridie ... inquit* (lines 11-12): which **two** of the following statements are true? Write down the letters for the correct ones.
      A   Julius caught sight of Helena
      B   Helena caught sight of Julius
      C   Helena said, 'I love you.'
      D   Julius said, 'I love you.'   [2]

11 *iuvenis ... placuerat* (lines 12-13):
    (i)   what **two** feelings did Julius have?   [2]
    (ii) why did he have the second of these feelings?   [4]

12 Translate *nam ... habitabant* (lines 13-14).   [11]

13 *postea ... aderat* (lines 14-16):
    (i)   when did Julius always look round?   [3]
    (ii) why did he do this?   [1]
    (iii) what do the words *illa semper aderat* suggest about Helena's thoughts?   [1]

14 *tandem ... amabat* (lines 16-17): how did Julius and Helena feel about each other?   [2]

15 *sed ... poterant* (line 18): what problem did Julius and Helena have? [2]

16 *Helena ... intrare* (lines 18-19): what **two** things could Helena not do?   [6]

17 *non ... volebat* (lines 19-20): which **two** of the following statements are true? Write down the letters for the correct ones.
      A   Helena wanted more than to see Julius in the street
      B   it was not satisfying for Julius to walk in the street
      C   Julius wanted Helena to be his girlfriend
      D   Helena wanted Julius to be her boyfriend   [2]

18 *mox ... nolebat* (lines 20-21):
    (i)   write down the Latin word that describes Helena.   [1]
    (ii) what did she refuse to do?   [2]
    (iii) why do you think she did this?   [1]

19 *post ... cupis* (lines 21-23):
    (i)   do the words *post paucos dies* suggest that Helena's parents were slow or quick to act? Give a reason for your answer. [1]
    (ii)   write down the Latin word that describes her parents. [1]
    (iii) translate *cur cenam non consumis*. [4]
    (iv) *num mortem cupis*: what do her parents suggest Helena might be wanting to do? [1]

20 *Helena ... nolo* (lines 23-25):
    (i)   what reason did Helena give for her action? [2]
    (ii)   write down and translate the Latin word that Helena uses to describe her parents. [2]
    (iii) which is the best translation of *vos me non sinitis eum etiam videre?*
        A   you also don't allow him to see me
        B   you also don't allow me to see him
        C   you don't allow him even to see me
        D   you don't allow me even to see him [1]
    (iv) what did Helena no longer want to do? [1]

21 *Helena ... lacrimans* (line 25): what did Helena do? [3]

22 *pater ... accipere* (lines 25-26): finish the sentence: 'Although her father was angry, he could do nothing other.............................' [2]

23 Which is the correct translation of *duo amantes erant laetissimi* (lines 26-27)?
        A   two of the lovers were happy
        B   the two lovers were happy
        C   the two lovers were very happy
        D   two of the lovers were very happy [1]

Total [100]

Section 2. Tests for WJEC Level 1 Additional

Introduction

These tests comprise stories that are purely for translation; it is this feature that makes these tests more demanding than the core ones. Accidence, syntax and defined vocabulary are the same as for the core tests. The storylines are also similar to those of the previous section. There is usually a slight gradient of difficulty, with harder linguistic elements tending to appear later in the stories. Students should aim for good English, without departing from a fairly literal rendering.

The mark schemes generally award two marks to each inflected Latin word, of which one is for the meaning and one is for the ending. Students should be reminded, therefore, that leaving blank spaces for unknown words is doubly costly; by guessing intelligently they can often earn one of the two available marks for each word. The commonest errors in translation at this level are wrong tenses of verbs and confusion between singular and plural nouns. Students should be advised, therefore, to double-check all such words at the end, to ensure consistency of sense.

1   *Caelius has a misunderstanding with his son.*

Caelius hortum <u>circumspectavit</u>; filium quaerebat. filius erat Quartus. Caelius Quartum conspicere non poterat. iratus erat, quod filium ad tabernam mittere volebat, nam omnes servi cum uxore iam exierant; itaque <u>nemo</u> alius erat qui ad tabernam ire poterat. Caelius <u>ipse</u> in domo manebat, amicum exspectans. Caelius amico <u>vinum</u> dare volebat, sed erat in domo nullum <u>vinum</u>. <u>necesse</u> erat Quarto <u>vinum</u> ferre.

'Quarte!' clamavit Caelius, 'ubi es? statim <u>huc</u> veni!' filius non respondit. Caelius etiam iratior erat. deinde amicus advenit. amicus, simulac Caelium salutavit, 'filium <u>tuum</u>,' inquit, 'in via ambulantem vidi.'

'quid?' Caelius dixit; 'puer <u>pessimus</u> est. in domo esse debet.'

Caelius, postquam e domo festinavit, filium conspexit.

'Quarte,' clamavit, 'in domum celeriter redi! te <u>punire</u> volo, quod ad tabernam ire non poteras. ubi tu eras?'

'sed pater,' respondit puer, 'mater me ad tabernam misit. <u>ecce</u> <u>vinum</u> quod mater rogavit.'

pater erat <u>attonitus</u>.

Names

Caelius, -i m.	Caelius	*Quartus, -i* m.	Quartus

Words

circumspecto, -are, -avi	I look round
nemo, nullius	no one
ipse, -a, -um	himself
vinum, -i n.	wine
necesse	necessary
huc	over here
tuus, -a, -um	your
pessimus, -a, -um	very bad
punio, -ire	I punish
ecce	here is
attonitus, -a, -um	astonished

2 *Septimus learns how his family came to be living in Britain.*

olim Septimus patri dixit: 'cur nos in Britannia habitamus? nos sumus Romani.'

pater risit. 'difficile est mihi omnia narrare,' respondit. 'ubi ego eram puer, in urbe Roma cum matre et patre habitabam. pater meus erat <u>legatus</u>. postquam Boudica multos Romanos <u>hic</u> necavit, <u>princeps</u> novam <u>legionem</u> in Britanniam misit. pater meus illam <u>legionem</u> per paucos <u>annos</u> ducebat. mater mea et ego ad hanc urbem cum patre venimus. tum, quod prope urbem erat <u>castellum</u>, nos in <u>praetorio</u> habitabamus. <u>cotidie</u> ego <u>milites</u> videbam. ubi pater in Italiam rediit, ego <u>nomen dedi</u>. in Britannia manere volebam, quod omnes amici <u>hic</u> erant. <u>legio</u> mea <u>hic</u> erat in urbe.'

Septimus, ubi hoc audivit, <u>attonitus</u> erat. 'num,' inquit, 'tu <u>miles</u> eras? id <u>nesciebam</u>.'

'<u>ita vero</u>,' respondit pater. 'deinde, ubi ex <u>exercitu</u> discessi, matrem tuam conspexi. <u>post</u> duos <u>annos</u>, tu <u>apparuisti</u>.'

Names

Septimus, -i m.	Septimus
Britannia, -ae f.	Britain
Romanus, -a, -um	Roman
Roma, -ae f.	Rome
Boudica, -ae f.	Boudica (a British queen)
Italia, -ae f.	Italy

Words

legatus, i m.	commander (of a legion)
hic	here
princeps, -ipis m.	emperor
legio, -onis f.	legion
annus, -i m.	year
castellum, -i n.	fort
praetorium, -i n.	commanding officer's house
cotidie	every day
miles, -itis m.	soldier
nomen do, dare, dedi	I join the army
attonitus, -a, -um	astonished
nescio, -ire	I do not know
ita vero	yes
exercitus, -us m. (abl. *-u*)	army
post + acc.	after
appareo, -ere, -ui	I appear

3 A powerful visitor persuades Flavius to sell a shop.

Flavius in <u>atrio</u> stabat. subito servus in <u>atrium</u> cucurrit.
'domine! domine!' clamavit servus.
'quid est?'
'homo ad ianuam stat. homo <u>aliquid</u> tibi dicere vult.'
'quis est ille homo?'
'<u>senator</u> est. <u>nomen</u> est Scipio.'
Flavius <u>anxius</u> erat; nam nullus <u>senator</u> ad domum <u>antea</u> venerat;
Scipio erat etiam vir <u>notissimus</u>. postquam servus <u>senatorem</u> in <u>atrium</u>
duxit, Flavius servum ei <u>vinum</u> ferre <u>iussit</u>.
'<u>salve</u>, <u>senator</u>,' inquit. 'quid vis?'
'nonne tu multas tabernas habes?'
'<u>ita vero</u>,' respondit Flavius, qui decem tabernas habebat.
'unam <u>emere</u> volo. <u>quantum</u> pecuniae <u>cupis</u>?'
Flavius, quod tabernam <u>vendere</u> nolebat, plus pecuniae quam <u>iustum</u>
erat rogavit. Scipio <u>pretium</u> statim accepit et discessit laetus. Flavius in
<u>atrio</u> sedebat ridens, quod <u>tantum</u> pecuniae acceperat.
<u>post</u> paucos <u>dies</u> tamen Flavius <u>rem</u> intellexit: illa taberna, quam
<u>senatori</u> <u>vendiderat</u>, multum <u>aurum</u> <u>celatum</u> habebat. hoc <u>aurum</u> per
multos <u>annos</u> in terra <u>sub</u> taberna <u>iacuerat</u>. Scipio solus de <u>auro</u>
<u>sciverat</u>.

Names

Flavius, -i m.	Flavius	*Scipio, -onis* m.	Scipio

Words

atrium, -i n.	main room	*vendo, -ere, -didi*	I sell
aliquid	something	*iustus, -a, -um*	reasonable
senator, -oris m.	senator	*pretium, -i* n.	price
nomen, -inis n.	name	*tantum* + gen.	so much
anxius, -a, -um	anxious	*post* + acc.	after
antea	previously	*dies, -ei* m.	day
notus, -a, -um	well-known	*res, rei* f.	the truth
vinum, -i n.	wine	*aurum, -i* n.	gold
iubeo, -ere, iussi	I order	*celatus, -a, -um*	hidden
salve	hello	*annus, -i* m.	year
ita vero	yes	*sub* + abl.	underneath
emo, -ere	I buy	*iaceo, -ere, -ui*	I lie
quantum + gen.	how much	*scio, -ire, -ivi*	I know
cupio, -ere	I want		

4 *Lucius benefits from his friend's misfortune.*

Lucius et Sextus erant amici. Lucius Sextum videre volebat. itaque Lucius ad Sextum servum misit. servus, 'dominus meus,' inquit, 'est anxius. tibi aliquid dare vult. statim ad forum ire debes.' itaque Lucius ad forum festinavit, et iam amicum quaerebat. tandem eum conspexit, vultum celantem.
    'cur tu vultum celas?' Lucius rogavit.
    'quod tres homines me petunt. me necare volunt,' respondit amicus.
    'quid tu fecisti?'
    'tabernam intravi, quod novam togam emere volebam. subito tres homines irruperunt, gladios tenentes. tabernarium omnem pecuniam tradere iusserunt. deinde clamaverunt: "nunc nobis statuam auream da." tabernarius, qui parere nolebat, ad ianuam tabernae cucurrit, sed homines eum crudeliter necaverunt. deinde statuam quaerebant. ubi homines me ad terram deiecerunt, perterritus eram. tum statuam conspexi; eam rapui et fugi. homines me viderunt et oppugnaverunt, sed me non ceperunt. iam me petunt. ecce statua. ego eam retinere nolo.'
    Lucius, qui statuam pulchriorem numquam viderat, laetissimus erat.

Names

Lucius, -i m.	Lucius	*Sextus, -i* m.	Sextus

Words

anxius, -a, -um	anxious	*tabernarius, -i* m.	shopkeeper
aliquid	something	*iubeo, -ere, iussi*	I order
forum, -i n.	forum, market place	*statua, -ae* f.	statue
		aureus, -a, -um	made of gold
vultus, -us m.	face	*pareo, -ere*	I obey
celo, -are	I hide	*deicio, -ere, -ieci*	I knock down
toga, -ae f.	toga	*rapio, -ere, -ui*	I grab
emo, -ere	I buy	*oppugno, -are, -avi*	I attack
irrumpo, -ere, -rupi	I burst in	*ecce*	here is
gladius, -i m.	sword	*retineo, -ere*	I keep

5a *A thief plans to steal a statue from a temple.*

prope mediam urbem erat templum Iovis. hoc templum erat antiquissimum et pulcherrimum. multi homines ex aliis partibus Italiae ad urbem veniebant, quod templum videre volebant. sacerdos, qui in templo laborabat, erat senex. hic vir saepe hospites in templum ducebat et monstrabat ingentem statuam dei, quae in medio templo stabat. statua erat aurea eburneaque. omnes, ubi statuam spectabant, formam artemque eius laudabant.

unus vir tamen aurum, non artem, amabat; hic vir erat fur. simulac statuam conspexit, eam surripere constituit. tres amicos habebat, qui fures quoque erant.

'cras,' inquit primus fur, 'mecum ad templum Iovis venite. plaustrum habere debemus; statuam dei in plaustrum ponere possumus.'

postridie quattuor homines per vias silentes urbis festinaverunt. media nox erat. nemo eos conspexit templum intrantes. fures erant laetissimi, ubi, faces tenentes, statuae appropinquaverunt.

Names

Iuppiter, Iovis, m.   Jupiter

Words

templum, -i n.	temple	*aurum, -i* n.	gold
antiquus, -a, -um	ancient	*fur, furis* m.	thief
pars, -tis f.	part	*surripio, -ere*	I steal
sacerdos, -otis m.	priest	*constituo, -ere, -ui*	I decide
hospes, -itis m.	visitor	*cras*	tomorrow
monstro, -are	I show	*plaustrum, -i* n.	cart
statua, -ae f.	statue	*postridie*	on the next day
aureus, -a, -um	made of gold	*silens, -ntis*	silent
eburneus, -a, -um	made of ivory	*nox, noctis* f.	night
forma, -ae f.	beauty	*nemo, nullius*	nobody
ars, artis f.	artistry	*fax, facis* f.	torch

5b *The statue is saved at the last moment.*

olim fur cum tribus amicis statuam dei surripere constituerat. iam in templo prope statuam stabant.
'quomodo statuam movere possumus?' rogavit unus ex amicis. 'statua est ingens.'
'sane difficile est,' respondit fur. 'sed bracchia et caput et crura divellere possumus. malleos habeo.'
fur amicis malleos tradidit. ubi unus amicus statuam tutudit, strepitus ingentissimus erat. homines perterriti erant.
'id facere non possumus,' inquit fur. 'periculosum est. statuam trudere debemus.'
quamquam fures cum omnibus viribus statuam truserunt, eam movere non potuerunt. subito vocem terribilem audiverunt:
'quid vos facitis, scelesti? cur statuam meam delere vultis? ego iam vobis mortem paro.'
fures e templo fugerunt perterriti. simulac fures discesserunt, sacerdos, qui in alia parte templi steterat, statuae appropinquavit.
'servus fidelis tibi sum, domine,' dixit sacerdos. 'quamquam sum senex, vox mea viridis est.'

Words

fur, furis m.	thief	*tundo, -ere, tutudi*	I strike
statua, -ae f.	statue	*strepitus, -us* m.	clang, noise
surripio, -ere	I steal	*periculosus, -a, -um*	dangerous
constituo, -ere, -i	I decide	*trudo, -ere, trusi*	I push
templum, -i n.	temple	*vires, -ium* f.pl.	strength
quomodo?	how?	*terribilis, -is, -e*	terrible
moveo, -ere	I move	*scelestus, -a, -um*	wicked
sane	certainly	*deleo, -ere*	I destroy
bracchium, -i n.	arm	*sacerdos, -otis* m.	priest
crus, cruris n.	leg	*pars, -tis* f.	part
divello, -ere	I break off	*fidelis, -is, -e*	faithful
malleus, -i m.	hammer	*viridis, -is, -e*	youthful

6 *Ambiorix finds husbands for his daughters.*

Ambiorix duas filias habebat, Iuliam et Corneliam. Ambiorix puellis maritos legere volebat. puellae tamen maritos habere nolebant, quod viros timebant. Ambiorix, quamquam <u>timorem</u> filiarum intellegebat, amicos ad cenam <u>invitavit</u>. postquam cibum consumpserunt, Ambiorix, 'amici,' inquit, 'ego maritos filiabus meis quaero. vos filios habetis. <u>quisquis</u> maximam <u>dotem</u> mihi <u>promittit</u>, uxorem legere potest.'

    <u>primo</u> amici nihil dixerunt; deinde unus, 'sed vir Romanus,' inquit, '<u>dotem</u> patri puellae non dat; pater puellae marito <u>dotem</u> dat.'

    '<u>verum</u> est,' respondit Ambiorix. 'sed ego Germanus sum; in Germania viri uxores <u>emunt</u>. filiae meae pulcherrimae sunt; itaque <u>aequum</u> est eas <u>vendere</u>. quis mihi <u>aurum</u> <u>promittere</u> vult?'

    tandem alius amicus, 'ego,' inquit, 'filium non habeo, sed uxor mea iam <u>mortua</u> est. novam uxorem quaero. Iulia mihi <u>placet</u>. <u>paratus</u> sum tibi <u>dotem</u> ingentem dare. <u>place</u>tne tibi?'

    'mihi <u>placet</u>,' respondit Ambiorix, 'sed quid de Cornelia? nonne illa quoque pulchra est?'

    mox alius amicus filium <u>proposuit</u>. Ambiorix laetus <u>consensit</u>.

Names

Ambiorix, -igis m.	Ambiorix
Iulia, -ae f.	Julia
Cornelia, -ae f.	Cornelia
Romanus, -a, -um	Roman
Germanus, -i m.	German
Germania, -ae f.	Germany

Words

timor, -oris m.	fear	*aequus, -a, -um*	reasonable
invito, -are, -avi	I invite	*vendo, -ere*	I sell
quisquis	whoever	*aurum, -i* n.	gold
dos, -tis f.	dowry (marriage gift)	*mortuus, -a, -um*	dead
		placeo, -ere + dat.	I please
promitto, -ere	I promise	*paratus, -a, -um*	ready
primo	at first	*propono, -ere, -posui*	I put forward
verus, -a, -um	true	*consentio, -ire, -sensi*	I agree
emo, -ere	I buy		

7 *Rufina does not appreciate her husband's choice of a new slave.*

Appius et Rufina in magna domo habitabant, sed paucos servos habebant. saepe necesse erat Rufinae cenam parare et ad tabernas ire, quod omnes servi alia faciebant. tandem Rufina irata marito dixit: 'cur tu alium servum non emis? ego amicas visitare volo, non in domo laborare. non sum ancilla.'

Appius, quamquam pecuniam impendere nolebat, consensit, quod uxorem amabat. itaque, ubi venalicius ad urbem venit, Appius ad eum festinavit. venalicius multos servos multasque ancillas habebat. Appius omnes inspexit. quamquam Rufina servum fortem emere voluerat, Appius ancillam pulcherrimam conspexit.

'hanc puellam emere volo,' venalicio dixit.

venalicius laetus erat, quod multam pecuniam accepit. Appius quoque laetissimus erat, quod puellam pulchriorem numquam viderat. Rufina tamen non erat laeta, quod e domo discedere non audebat: nam maritum cum ancilla in domo relinquere nolebat.

Names

Appius, -i m.	Appius
Rufina, -ae f.	Rufina

Words

necesse	necessary
emo, -ere	I buy
amica, -ae f.	(female) friend
visito, -are	I visit
impendo, -ere	I spend
consentio, -ire, -sensi	I agree
venalicius, -i m.	slave-dealer
inspicio, -ere, -spexi	I inspect
audeo, -ere	I dare
relinquo, -ere	I leave

8a *Domitius saves a young man's life.*

Domitius erat nuntius. Domitius semper diligenter laborabat. longa itinera faciebat, epistulas portans, quas imperator scripserat. interdiu equitabat, noctu in mansionibus dormiebat; ita epistulae ad homines, qui eas exspectabant, semper celeriter adveniebant.

olim iter longissimum faciebat, nam imperator eum cum epistulis ad principes Gallorum miserat. magna pars itineris per silvas iacebat. nullus alius erat in via. subito Domitius clamores audivit. vox hominis clamabat: 'me adiuva! me adiuva!' Domitius de equo statim desiluit et per arbores cucurrit. mox iuvenem conspexit, ad arborem ligatum. iuvenis perterritus et debilis erat, nam diu ibi fuerat. Domitius eum celeriter liberavit et ei aquam cibumque dedit. iuvenis, simulac vires recepit, rem narravit.

'ubi,' inquit iuvenis, 'ego per has silvas equitabam, subito quattuor latrones me oppugnaverunt. postquam me superaverunt et ad arborem ligaverunt, equum et omnem pecuniam abstulerunt. felix sum quod me non necaverunt. etiam felicior sum, quod tu me nunc liberavisti.'

Names

Domitius, -i m.	Domitius
Galli, -orum m.pl.	the Gauls

Words

nuntius, -i m.	messenger	*desilio, -ire, -silui*	I jump down
diligenter	carefully, hard	*arbor, -oris* f.	tree
longus, -a, -um	long	*ligatus, -a, -um*	tied
imperator, -oris m.	emperor	*debilis, -is, -e*	weak
interdiu	by day	*ibi*	there
equito, -are	I ride (a horse)	*vires, -ium* f.pl.	strength
noctu	at night	*recipio, -ere, -cepi*	I recover
mansio, -onis f.	roadside inn	*res, rei* f.	story
princeps, -ipis m.	chieftain	*latro, -onis* m.	robber
silva, -ae f.	wood	*oppugno, -are, -avi*	I attack
iaceo, -ere	I lie	*ligo, -are, avi*	I tie
clamor, -oris m.	shout	*aufero, -re, abstuli*	I steal
adiuvo, -are	I help	*felix, -icis*	lucky
equus, -i m.	horse		

8b *Domitius and the young man recover their stolen property.*

Domitius per silvas iter faciebat. Domitius, ubi iuvenem invenit, quem latrones ad arborem ligaverant, eum liberavit. postquam Domitius iuveni cibum aquamque dedit, ad viam redierunt. equum tamen Domitii conspicere non potuerunt. Domitius iratus erat, quod equus epistulas imperatoris portabat.

difficile quoque erat iuveni ambulare, quod debilis erat. iuvenis et Domitius prope viam sedebant, consilium quaerentes.

'quid facere debemus?' Domitius rogavit. 'per tantas silvas ambulare non possumus.'

'ubi iter heri faciebam,' respondit iuvenis, 'ad vicum veni. ille vicus prope est. fortasse aliquis nos adiuvare potest.'

itaque duo viri per tres horas ambulaverunt. ubi vico appropinquaverunt, iuvenis subito dixit: 'hominem, qui me ad arborem ligavit, domum intrantem conspicio.' Domitius iuvenem e via in silvas statim traxit. ibi manebant. simulac nox fuit, in domum irruperunt et latronem superaverunt. deinde omnia, quae latrones abstulerant, receperunt.

Names

Domitius, -i m.   Domitius

Words

silva, -ae f.	wood	*vicus, -i* m.	village
invenio, -ire, -veni	I find	*fortasse*	perhaps
latro, -onis m.	robber	*aliquis*	somebody
arbor, -oris f.	tree	*adiuvo, -are*	I help
ligo, -are, -avi	I tie	*hora, -ae* f.	hour
equus, -i m.	horse	*ibi*	there
imperator, -oris m.	emperor	*nox, noctis* f.	night
debilis, -is, -e	weak	*irrumpo, -ere, -rupi*	I burst in
consilium, -i n.	plan	*aufero, -re, abstuli*	I steal
tantus, -a, -um	such great	*recipio, -ere, -cepi*	I get back

Section 3. Tests for OCR Foundation Tier

Introduction

These are three-part momentum tests, with the first and third sections tested by comprehension questions and the second by translation. Accidence, syntax and vocabulary are all based on the GCSE specification, while the format of the tests is closely modelled on that of the GCSE Foundation Tier Paper 1. There are no separate tests based on Paper 2 because the only real difference between Paper 1 and Paper 2 is the amount of defined vocabulary candidates are expected to know: 350 as opposed to 200 words. Other differences, such as subject matter and the fact that Paper 2 comprises two sections only, are relatively insignificant.

Only five tests have been included in this section, because of lack of space. Teachers considering entering students for the Foundation Tier GCSE are advised to use some of the more demanding tests in the later sections as preparation, once they have completed the five tests here. Marking of the translation requires the passage to be divided into five sections, each to be marked out of 4, according to the proportion of sense. The storylines are more or less the same as some of those used in Sections 1 and 5 (three from daily life and two from mythology), the assumption being that it is unlikely that the same students will be entered for both the Level 1 / 2 and the Foundation Tier GCSE.

1 Section A: Read the passages and answer the questions.

Clemens takes his son on his first visit to the baths.

1 Claudia erat filia Clementis. Clemens filium quoque habebat; nomen
2 eius erat Septimus. olim Clemens Septimo dixit, 'mecum veni. iam
3 <u>tempus</u> est tibi ad <u>thermas</u> ire, quod iuvenis es, non puer.' Septimus
4 laetus erat, quod <u>numquam</u> <u>antea</u> <u>thermas</u> intraverat. Claudia tamen
5 patri dixit se quoque <u>thermas</u> <u>visitare</u> velle. 'egone,' inquit, 'vobiscum
6 venire possum?' 'non potes, filia,' respondit Clemens. 'si tu <u>thermas</u>
7 videre vis, <u>necesse</u> est tibi cum matre ire. ego solos iuvenes in
8 <u>thermas</u> ducere possum.' mox Septimus et pater laete e villa exierunt
9 ut ad <u>thermas</u> irent.

Names

Claudia, -ae f.	Claudia
Clemens, -entis m.	Clemens
Septimus, -i m.	Septimus

Vocabulary

tempus, -oris n.	time	*antea*	before
thermae, -arum f.pl.	baths	*visito, -are*	I visit
numquam	never	*necesse*	necessary

1 Who was Claudia (line 1)? [2]

2 *Clemens ... Septimus* (lines 1-2): who was Septimus? [1]

3 Which is the correct translation of *olim Clemens Septimo dixit* (line 2)?
    A when Clemens said to Septimus
    B once Clemens said to Septimus
    C once Septimus said to Clemens [1]

4 *mecum veni* (line 2): what did Clemens tell Septimus to do? [2]

5 *iam ... puer* (lines 2-3):
    (i) what did Clemens say it was time for Septimus to do? [1]
    (ii) what reason did he give for this? [2]

6 *Septimus ... intraverat* (lines 3-4): why was Septimus happy? [2]

7 *Claudia ... possum* (lines 4-6): what did Claudia ask her father? [3]

8   *si ... possum* (lines 6-8):
    (i)   what did Clemens say Claudia ought to do if she wanted to see
          the baths?   [2]
    (ii) what reason did Clemens give for not being able to take her?   [3]

9   *mox ... irent* (lines 8-9): why did Clemens and Septimus leave the
    house?   [1]

The activities of a family slave, however, cause problems.

servus quoque ibat. <u>thermae</u> maximae erant. ubi intraverunt, Septimus
<u>attonitus</u> erat, quod <u>palaestra</u> erat <u>plena</u> hominum currentium
clamantiumque. Clemens filium in <u>apodyterium</u> duxit. <u>vestes</u> servo
dederunt, quem iusserunt eas <u>custodire</u>. omnes <u>partes</u> <u>thermarum</u>
<u>visitaverunt</u>. tandem Clemens Septimo dixit, 'nunc exibimus; mater tua
nos exspectat.'

Vocabulary

thermae, -arum f.pl.	baths	*vestes, -ium* f. pl.	clothes
attonitus, -a, -um	astonished	*custodio, -ire*	I guard
palaestra, -ae f.	exercise area	*pars, -tis* f.	part
plenus, -a, -um	full	*visito, -are, -avi*	I visit
apodyterium, -i n.	changing room		

10   Translate the above passage into good English.   [20]

Section A Total [40]

Section B: Read the passage and answer the questions.

Clemens is made even angrier.

1   cum in <u>apodyterium</u> rediissent, nec <u>vestes</u> nec servum videre
2   poterant. Clemens iratissimus erat. ei <u>necesse</u> erat <u>novas</u> <u>tunicas</u>
3   <u>quaerere</u>. ubi e <u>thermis</u> exierunt, Clemens filiam et matrem eius vidit.
4   'laetissimae sumus,' inquit Claudia, 'quod in <u>thermis</u> servus tuus hunc
5   <u>anulum</u> <u>aureum</u> <u>invenit</u>.' 'ubi est servus?' Clemens rogavit. 'ego eum
6   ad tabernam misi,' respondit <u>uxor</u>. iam Clemens erat <u>etiam</u> iratior.

Vocabulary

apodyterium, -i n.	changing room	*thermae, -arum* f.pl.	baths
vestes, -ium f. pl.	clothes	*anulus, -i* m.	ring
necesse	necessary	*aureus, -a, -um*	gold
novus, -a, -um	new	*invenio, -ire, -veni*	I find
tunica, -ae f.	tunic	*uxor, -oris* f.	wife
quaero, -ere	I look for	*etiam*	even

11 *cum ... poterant* (lines 1-2): describe fully what happened when
    Clemens and Septimus returned to the changing room. [4]

12 *Clemens ... quaerere* (lines 2-3):
    (i)   how did Clemens feel? [2]
    (ii) what did he have to do? [1]

13 *ubi ... vidit* (line 3): whom did Clemens see on leaving the baths? [2]

14 *laetissimae ... invenit* (lines 4-5): according to Claudia, why were
    she and her mother very happy? [4]

15 *ubi ... iratior* (lines 5-6):
    (i)   what did Clemens want to know? [1]
    (ii) which is the correct translation of *ego eum ad tabernam misi*
          (lines 5-6)?
          A   he sent me to the shop
          B   I was miserable in that shop
          C   I sent him to the shop [1]

    (iii) how did Clemens feel at the end of the story? [1]

16 For each of the two following Latin words, give **one** English word
    which has been derived from the Latin word **and** give the meaning
    of the English word.
    custodire
    servus. [4]

Section B Total [20]
Paper Total [60]

2 Section A: Read the passages and answer the questions.

The world is ruled by the Titans, of whom the strongest is Cronus. Cronus is afraid of an oracle that has predicted a dreadful future for him.

1 Cronus erat Titanus. Cronus <u>uxorem</u> habebat, Rheam nomine.
2 Rhea Cronum et amabat et timebat; nam ille ferox erat. ubi filia <u>nata</u>
3 <u>est</u>, Rhea laeta erat; <u>infanti</u> pulchrae nomen Vestam dedit. Cronus
4 tamen erat iratus, quod <u>oraculum</u> audiverat: '<u>liberi</u> tui,' inquit <u>oraculum</u>,
5 'te necabunt.' itaque Cronus hoc facere constituit: ubi Rhea ei Vestam
6 dedit ut eam teneret, eam statim consumpsit. quamquam Cronus iam
7 laetior erat, Rhea perterrita erat. ubi paucos post annos filius <u>natus est</u>,
8 Cronus eum quoque consumpsit. hoc <u>modo</u> tres <u>alii</u> <u>liberi</u>, ubi <u>nati sunt</u>,
9 necati sunt.

Names

Cronus, -i m.	Cronus	*Titanus, -i* m.	Titan
Rhea, -ae f.	Rhea	*Vesta, -ae* f.	Vesta

Vocabulary

uxor, -oris f.	wife	*liberi, -orum* m.pl.	children
natus, -a est	was born	*modus, -i* m.	way
infans, -ntis m. / f.	baby	*alius, -a, -ud*	other
oraculum, -i n.	oracle (a prediction of the future)	*nati sunt*	were born

1   *Cronus ... Titanus* (line 1): what are we told here about Cronus?   [1]

2   Who was Rhea (line 1)?   [1]

3   *Rhea ... erat* (line 2):
     (i)   what **two** feelings did Rhea have towards Cronus?   [2]
     (ii)   why did she have the second of these feelings?   [1]

4   *ubi ... dedit* (lines 2-3): why was Rhea happy?   [1]

5   *Cronus ... necabunt* (lines 3-5): why was Cronus angry? Give full
     details.   [3]

6   *ubi ... consumpsit* (lines 5-6):
     (i)   what did Cronus do?   [2]
     (ii)   when did he do this?   [4]

67

7   Which is the correct translation of *Cronus iam laetior erat* (lines 6-7)?
    A   now Cronus was happy
    B   now Cronus was happier
    C   now Cronus was very happy
    D   now Cronus was the happiest   [1]

8   *Rhea perterrita erat* (line 7): how did Rhea feel?   [1]

9   *ubi ... necati sunt* (lines 7-9):
    (i)   when was a son born?   [2]
    (ii) how many children did Cronus and Rhea have altogether
          in this first part of the story?   [1]

    Rhea devises a plan to fool Cronus.

    Rhea, postquam filius <u>alius</u> tandem <u>natus est</u>, cui nomen Iovem dedit,
    eum servare constituit. primum matri et patri <u>infantem</u> dedit; deinde,
    cum Cronus advenisset filium rogans, ei <u>saxum</u> <u>vestibus</u> <u>involutum</u>
    dedit et tam <u>vehementer</u> clamabat, ut Cronus <u>saxum</u> consumeret
    <u>ignarus</u>. postquam Cronus abiit, Rhea cucurrit ut filium teneret.

Name

Iuppiter, Iovis m.   Jupiter

Vocabulary

alius, -a, -ud	another	*vestes, -ium* f. pl.	clothes
natus est	was born	*involutus, -a, -um*	wrapped
infans, -ntis m. / f.	baby	*vehementer*	loudly
saxum, -i n.	stone	*ignarus, -a, -um*	without realising

10 Translate the above passage into good English.   [20]

Section A Total [40]

Section B: Read the passage and answer the questions.

Cronus is defeated.

1 Iuppiter, ubi <u>adultus</u> erat, Cronum <u>punire</u> volebat. optimum vinum
2 Crono dedit. Cronus, ubi vinum <u>bibit</u>, plus vini rogavit. mox tantum vini
3 <u>biberat</u>, ut omnia quae in <u>ventre</u> tenebantur <u>evomeret</u>. omnia <u>fragmenta</u>
4 quinque <u>liberorum</u>, quos consumpserat, <u>eiecta sunt</u>. haec <u>fragmenta</u>
5 <u>cohaeserunt</u>; mox tres feminae duoque viri prope Iovem stabant.
6 Cronus <u>attonitus</u> fuit. 'qui vos estis?' inquit. 'nos sumus tui <u>liberi</u>,' illi
7 responderunt. 'iam te necabimus.'

Vocabulary

adultus, -a, -um	grown up	*fragmentum, -i* n.	fragment, piece
punio, -ire	I punish		
bibo, -ere, bibi	I drink	*liberi, -orum* m.pl.	children
venter, ventris m.	stomach	*eicio, -ere, -ieci, -iectus*	I throw out
evomo, -ere	I vomit up, spew out	*cohaereo, -ere, -haesi*	I clump together
		attonitus, -a, -um	astonished

11 *Iuppiter ... volebat* (line 1): how did Jupiter feel when he had grown up? [2]

12 *optimum ... rogavit* (lines 1-2):
   (i)   what did Jupiter give to Cronus? [2]
   (ii) how do we know that Cronus liked what he was given? [2]

13 *mox ... evomeret* (lines 2-3):
   (i)   which is the correct translation of *mox tantum vini biberat*?
       A soon he was drinking so much wine
       B soon he drank so much wine
       C soon he had drunk so much wine
       D soon so much wine was drunk [1]
   (ii) what did Cronus vomit up? [2]

14 *omnia ... sunt* (lines 3-4): of what did the *fragmenta* consist? [2]

15 *haec ... stabant* (lines 4-5): describe the transformation that took place. [4]

16 *iam te necabimus* (line 7): what threat was made? [1]

69

17 For each of the two following Latin words, give **one** English word
which has been derived from the Latin word **and** give the meaning
of the English word.
optimum
vinum. [4]

Section B Total [20]
Paper Total [60]

3 **Section A:** Read the passages and answer the questions.

Helen tries to help her friend to gain a better life.

1 Helena in pulchra villa habitabat. pater Helenae multos servos
2 multasque ancillas habebat, quarum una erat puella, Phoebe.
3 quamquam Phoebe in villa laborare <u>debebat</u>, Helena et Phoebe erant
4 <u>amicae</u>; multa <u>una</u> faciebant. Helena, cum esset puella, ad <u>ludum</u> cum
5 <u>fratribus</u> non ibat. pater eius, qui vir <u>dives</u> erat, unum ex servis eam
6 docere iusserat. hic servus <u>legere</u> poterat. olim Helena patrem rogavit
7 cur servus Phoeben quoque non doceret; dixit Phoeben <u>intellegentem</u>
8 esse. 'nonne,' inquit, 'ancilla <u>docta</u> maiorem <u>valorem</u> habet?' pater,
9 quod filiam amabat, <u>consensit</u>.

Names

Helena, -ae f.	Helena
Phoebe, -es (acc. *–en*)	Phoebe

Vocabulary

debeo, -ere	I have to, must	*lego, -ere*	I read
amica, -ae f.	friend	*intellegens, -ntis*	intelligent
una	together	*doctus, -a, -um*	educated
ludus, -i m.	school	*valor, -oris* m.	value
frater, -ris m.	brother	*consentio, -ire, -sensi*	I agree
dives, -itis	rich		

1 *Helena ... habitabat* (line 1): where did Helena live? [1]

2 *pater ... habebat* (lines 1-2): what did Helena's father have? [3]

3 *quarum ... Phoebe* (line 2): give two details about Phoebe. [2]

4   *Helena ... faciebant* (lines 3-4): how did Phoebe and Helena show
    that they were friends?   [2]

5   *Helena ... ibat* (lines 4-5):
    (i)   what did Helena not do?   [2]
    (ii) what reason is given for this?   [1]

6   *pater ... iusserat* (lines 5-6): what had Helena's father ordered a
    slave to do?   [1]

7   *hic servus legere poterat* (line 6): which is the correct translation
    of these words?
                A   the slave could choose this
                B   the slave could read this
                C   this slave could choose
                D   this slave could read   [1]

8   *olim ... doceret* (lines 6-7): what did Helena ask her father?   [3]

9   *dixit ... habet* (lines 7-9): what were the two arguments that Helena
    used to try to persuade her father?   [4]

Phoebe becomes dissatisfied with her life.

tres annos servus duas puellas plurima docebat. sed Phoebe, cum
<u>etiam</u> nunc in villa laboraret, erat tristis. olim <u>aberat</u>. pater Helenam
iussit eam <u>quaerere</u>. ubi Helena Phoeben vidit in horto sedentem, eam
rogavit cur non laboraret. 'non laboro,' illa respondit, 'quod iam <u>legere</u>
et scribere possum. laborare non volo.'

Vocabulary

etiam	even
absum, -esse	I am absent
quaero, -ere	I look for
lego, -ere	I read

10   Translate the above passage into good English.   [20]

Section A Total [40]

Section B: Read the passage and answer the questions.

Helena helps her friend again.

1 Helena ad patrem ivit ut ei narraret quid Phoebe dixisset. pater iam
2 iratior erat, quod servos <u>ignavos</u> habere nolebat. 'pater <u>carissime</u>,'
3 inquit Helena <u>suaviter</u> ridens, 'nonne Phoebe <u>docta</u> est? tibi <u>necesse</u>
4 est ei <u>laborem</u> meliorem dare.' quid <u>aliud</u> pater facere potuit? mox, ubi
5 pater amicis cenam dabat, Phoebe <u>carmina</u> <u>recitabat</u>. pater iam laetus
6 erat, quod ab omnibus amicis laudabatur. Phoebe quoque erat laeta.

Vocabulary

ignavus, -a, -um	lazy	*necesse*	necessary
carus, -a, -um	dear	*labor, -oris* m.	work
suaviter	sweetly	*carmen, -inis* n.	poem
doctus, -a, -um	educated	*recito, -are*	I read aloud

11 *Helena ... dixisset* (line 1): why did Helena go to her father? [3]

12 *pater iam ... nolebat* (lines 1-2):
  (i) how did Helena's father feel? [1]
  (ii) why did he feel like this? [2]

13 *pater carissime ... est* (lines 2-3):
  (i) which word best describes Helena's actions and words? Write
     down your chosen letter **and** give a reason for your answer.
     A coaxing
     B anxious
     C angry
     D hostile [1]

  (ii) which is the correct translation of *nonne Phoebe docta est*?
     A Phoebe isn't educated, is she?
     B is Phoebe educated?
     C is Phoebe educated, or isn't she?
     D Phoebe is educated, isn't she? [1]

14 *tibi ... dare* (lines 3-4): what did Helena say her father should do? [2]

15 *quid aliud pater facere potuit* (line 4): what do these words
  suggest about the relations between Helena and her father? [1]

16 *mox ... recitabat* (lines 4-5):
   (i)   what did Phoebe now do to help Helena's father?   [1]
   (ii) when did she do this?   [2]

17 *pater ... laeta* (lines 5-6): why were Helena's father and Phoebe
    happy? Give one reason for each.   [2]

18 For each of the two following Latin words, give **one** English word
    which has been derived from the Latin word **and** give the meaning
    of the English word.
    narraret
    amicis.   [4]

Section B Total [20]
Paper Total [60]

4 Section A: Read the passages and answer the questions.

*At the end of the Trojan War, Aeneas, who is a member of the royal
family of Troy, gathers together the Trojan survivors and sails away to
establish a new home. They are blown off course.*

1 Aeneas erat <u>princeps</u> Troianus. Aeneas, postquam Graeci urbem
2 eius ceperunt, cum patre et filio et omnibus <u>aliis</u>, a Graecis non
3 necatis, ab urbe fugerat. iam <u>navigabant</u>, ut <u>novam</u> urbem <u>conderent</u>.
4 sed <u>tempestas</u> ingens naves ad Africam <u>pepulit</u>. cum navis in qua
5 Aeneas <u>navigabat</u> ad terram advenisset, Aeneas laetissimus erat quod
6 pater et filius non necati erant. <u>ceteras</u> naves tamen <u>deletas</u> esse
7 <u>putabat</u>. Aeneas <u>collem</u> ascendit, ut <u>circumspectaret</u>. <u>auxilium</u> enim
8 <u>petere</u> volebat, sed neque urbem neque homines videre poterat.
9 subito puella pulcherrima ad eum venit.

Names

Aeneas, -ae m.	Aeneas	*Troianus, -a, -um*	Trojan
Graeci, -orum m.pl.	the Greeks	*Africa, -ae* f.	Africa

Vocabulary

princeps, -ipis m.	prince	*tempestas, -atis* f.	storm
alius, -a, -ud	other	*pello, -ere, pepuli*	I drive
navigo, -are	I sail	*ceteri, -ae, -a*	the rest (of)
novus, -a, -um	new	*deleo, -ere, -evi, -etus*	I destroy
condo, -ere	I found, build	*puto, -are*	I think

73

collis, -is m.	hill	*auxilium, -i* n.	help
circumspecto, -are	I look round	*peto, -ere*	I look for

1   *Aeneas, postquam ... fugerat* (lines 1-3):
   (i)   what happened to Troy? [2]
   (ii)   what **two** members of his family accompanied Aeneas? [2]
   (iii)   which other people accompanied him? [2]
   (iv)   which is the correct translation of *ab urbe fugerat*?
       A   they had fled from the city
       B   he fled from the city
       C   they fled from the city
       D   he had fled from the city [1]

2   *sed ... pepulit* (line 4): how did their plans go wrong? [2]

3   *cum ... necati erant* (lines 4-6):
   (i)   which ship reached land? [1]
   (ii)   why did Aeneas feel very happy? [3]

4   *ceteras ... putabat* (lines 6-7): how do you think this would have made Aeneas feel? Give a reason for your answer. [2]

5   *auxilium ... poterat* (lines 7-8):
   (i)   what did Aeneas wish to do? [1]
   (ii)   what tells us this would be difficult? [2]

6   *subito ... venit* (line 9): who suddenly came up to Aeneas? [2]

Aeneas learns about the land and its people.

Aeneas puellam rogavit <u>num</u> ab urbe <u>propinqua</u> venisset.
    puella, '<u>ita vero</u>,' respondit. 'Carthago est <u>nova</u> urbs, quam <u>regina</u> Dido aedificat. Dido cum multis civibus a <u>patria</u> fugit, quod <u>frater</u> eam necare volebat, ut <u>ipse</u> rex esset. sed quis es tu?'
    Aeneas dixit se quoque <u>coactum esse</u> <u>patriam</u> <u>relinquere</u>.

Names

Carthago, -inis f.	Carthage	*Dido, -onis* f.	Dido

Vocabulary

num	whether	*frater, -ris* m.	brother
propinquus, -a, -um	nearby	*ipse, -a, -um*	himself
ita vero	yes	*cogo, -ere, -egi, -actus*	I force
novus, -a, -um	new	*relinquo, -ere*	I leave
regina, -ae f.	queen		behind
patria, -ae f.	homeland		

7   Translate the above passage into good English.   [20]

Section A Total [40]

Section B: Read the passage and answer the questions.

Queen Dido welcomes Aeneas and his people.

1   Aeneas, postquam ad suos rediit, cum paucis amicis ad urbem
2   Didonis ambulavit. ubi urbem intrabant, multos homines viderunt
3   templa, forum et villas aedificantes. in medio stabat Dido. <u>regina</u>, cum
4   nuntiatum esset Aeneam, <u>principem</u> Troianum, advenisse, laetissima
5   erat. 'nos multa de <u>bello</u> Troiano et de <u>virtute</u> Aeneae audivimus.
6   cenam optimam vobis parabimus.' Aeneas <u>ceteros</u> suos a nave
7   <u>arcessivit</u>.

Vocabulary

regina, -ae f.	queen	*virtus, -utis* f.	courage
princeps, -ipis m.	prince	*ceteri, -ae, -a*	the rest (of)
bellum, -i n.	war	*arcesso, -ere, -ivi*	I send for

8   *Aeneas ... ambulavit* (lines 1-2):
    (i)   what did Aeneas do first?   [2]
    (ii)   where did he walk to?   [1]
    (iii) which is the correct translation of *cum* (line 1)?
           A   with
           B   since
           C   although
           D   when   [1]

75

9 *ubi ... aedificantes* (lines 2-3):
  (i)   when did they see many men?   [1]
  (ii) what were the men building?   [3]

10 *in medio stabat Dido* (line 3): where was Dido standing?   [1]

11 *regina ... erat* (lines 3-5):
  (i)   what was announced?   [2]
  (ii) how did Dido react to the announcement?   [1]

12 *nos ... parabimus* (lines 5-6):
  (i)   what had the people of Carthage heard much about?   [2]
  (ii) what would they now prepare for the Trojans?   [2]

13 For each of the two following Latin words, give **one** English word
   which has been derived from the Latin word **and** give the meaning
   of the English word.
   medios
   nave.   [4]

Section B Total [20]
Paper Total [60]

5 **Section A:**   Read the passages and answer the questions.

   A priest promises that the goddess Isis will protect the city.

1   Octavius erat <u>sacerdos</u> deae Isidis. multi cives Isidem <u>colebant</u>,
2   quod dea <u>aliam</u> <u>vitam</u> post mortem <u>promittebat</u>.
3   iam <u>ver</u> advenerat. <u>sacerdotes</u> <u>pompam</u> per mediam urbem
4   ducebant, <u>statuam</u> deae portantes. cives omnes in viis stabant, ut eam
5   spectarent.
6   <u>sacerdotes</u>, cum in medium forum venissent, <u>statuam</u> in terra
7   <u>posuerunt</u>. tum <u>principes</u> ad <u>statuam</u> venerunt, <u>dona</u> portantes. 'da
8   nobis bonam <u>fortunam</u> ac <u>frumentum</u> plurimum,' rogaverunt <u>principes</u>.
9   Octavius, quod erat <u>dux</u> <u>sacerdotum</u>, <u>pro</u> dea respondit. 'dea,' inquit,
10 'dicit se hanc urbem semper servaturam esse. dea civibus optimam
11 <u>fortunam</u> dabit.'

Names

Octavius, -i m.   Octavius   *Isis, -idis* f.   Isis (a goddess)

76

Vocabulary

sacerdos, -otis m.	priest	*pono, -ere, posui*	I place
colo, -ere	I worship	*princeps, -ipis* m.	leading citizen
alius, -a, -ud	another	*donum, -i* n.	gift
vita, -ae f.	life	*fortuna, -ae* f.	fortune
promitto, -ere	I promise	*frumentum, -i* n.	corn
ver, veris n.	spring	*dux, ducis* m.	leader
pompa, -ae f.	procession	*pro* + abl.	on behalf of
statua, -ae f.	statue		

1   What do we learn about Octavius in line 1?   [2]

2   *multi ... promittebat* (lines 1-2):
   (i)   how popular was the worship of Isis?   [1]
   (ii) why was this?   [2]

3   Which is the correct translation of *iam ver advenerat* (line 3)?
      A   now spring was approaching
      B   now spring had arrived
      C   for spring was coming
      D   now it was approaching spring   [1]

4   *sacerdotes ... portantes* (lines 3-4): what **two** things were the priests
   doing?   [4]

5   *cives ... spectarent* (lines 4-5): what did the citizens wish to do?   [2]

6   *sacerdotes ... posuerunt* (lines 6-7): where was the statue placed?
   Give **two** details.   [2]

7   *da ... principes* (lines 7-8): what did the leading citizens pray for?   [2]

8   *dea ... dabit* (lines 9-11): what **two** promises did Octavius make on behalf
   of the goddess?   [4]

Peter objects to the worship of Isis.

omnes cives erant laetissimi. sed erat unus vir, Petrus, qui, cum esset
Christianus, <u>alios</u> deos videre nolebat; Christo soli <u>credebat</u>. Petrus tam
iratus erat ut <u>inter</u> <u>principes</u> curreret. 'Isis non est dea,' clamavit.
'Christus solus vos servare potest. Christum, non Isidem, <u>colite</u>.'

Names

Petrus, -i m.	Peter	*Christianus, -i* m.	Christian
Christus, -i m.	Christ		

Vocabulary

alius, -a, -ud	other
credo, -ere + dat.	I believe in
inter + acc.	among
princeps, -ipis m.	leading citizen
colo, -ere	I worship

9   Translate the above passage into good English.   [20]

Section A Total [40]

Section B: Read the passage and answer the questions.

Peter fails in his attempt to persuade the people to accept Christ.

1   <u>principes</u>, 'abi,' clamaverunt. 'Isis est optima dea. de tuo deo audire
2   nolumus.' tum Petrus, 'in nomine Christi,' respondit, 'vobis omnibus
3   <u>maledico</u>. Christus vos <u>puniet</u>.' <u>principes</u>, postquam haec audiverunt,
4   hominem captum in <u>carcerem</u> traxerunt.
5   mox erat tanta <u>tempestas</u>, ut multi cives necarentur. Petrus, cum
6   hoc <u>cognovisset</u>, risit. 'meus deus,' inquit, 'vos <u>punivit</u>, <u>sicut</u> dixi.'
7   <u>principes</u> irati responderunt se deum tam <u>crudelem</u> non <u>culturos esse</u>.

Vocabulary

princeps, -ipis m.	leading citizen		*tempestas, -atis* f.	storm
maledico, -ere + dat.	I curse		*cognosco, -ere, -novi*	I learn
punio, -ire, -ivi	I punish		*sicut*	just as
carcer, -eris m.	prison		*crudelis, -is, -e*	cruel
			colo, -ere, -ui, cultus	I worship

10 *principes, 'abi,' clamaverunt* (line 1): what did the leading citizens
     tell Peter to do?   [1]

11 *Isis est optima dea* (line 1): how is Isis described?   [1]

78

12 Which is the correct translation of *de tuo deo audire nolumus* (lines 1-2)?
    A we don't want to hear about your god
    B your god doesn't want to listen to us
    C we want to listen to your god
    D our god doesn't want to hear about you   [1]

13 *tum ... puniet* (lines 2-3); how did Peter reply to the leaders? Make **two** points.   [4]

14 *principes ... traxerunt* (lines 3-4): what happened to Peter?   [2]

15 *mox ... necarentur* (line 5): what happened as a result of the storm? [2]

16 *Petrus ... risit* (lines 5-6): how did Peter react to the news?   [1]

17 *meus ... dixi* (line 6): how did Peter explain the event?   [2]

18 *principes ... esse* (line 7): how did the leading citizens reply?   [2]

19 For each of the two following Latin words, give **one** English word which has been derived from the Latin word **and** give the meaning of the English word.
nomine
captum.   [4]

Section B Total [20]
Paper Total [60]

Section 4. Tests for OCR Higher Tier

Introduction

These three-part momentum tests are identical in format to those for the Foundation Tier in the previous section. The differences between the two tiers consist in the larger vocabulary list (an additional 100 words) and a few extra constructions required for the Higher Tier. Only five tests have been included in this section, again because of lack of space. Teachers considering entering students for the Higher Tier GCSE are advised to use the more demanding tests in the final section as preparation, once they have completed the five tests here. The storylines are more or less the same as some of those used in Sections 2 and 5 (historical); there are sufficient differences, however, to make it worth giving the second version to students to tackle, after an appropriate time interval. Marking is the same as for the previous section.

1 Section A: Read the passages and answer the questions.

There is a dispute over who should be king of Alba Longa.

1 Numitor et Amulius erant filii regis Albae Longae. post mortem patris
2 eorum, Numitor, cum <u>senior</u> esset, credebat se regem futurum esse.
3 Amulius tamen, qui vir crudelis erat, fratrem ex urbe <u>expulit</u> ut rex ipse
4 esset. deinde Amulius, filiis Numitoris necatis, filiam eius, Rheam
5 Silviam nomine, <u>coegit</u> Virginem Vestalem esse, ne filium <u>pareret</u>; nam
6 eo tempore Virgo Vestalis, si cum viro dormiverat, necata est.
7   quamquam Amulius tantum fecit, ut <u>aemulos</u> <u>removeret</u>, Rhea Silvia
8 duos filios <u>peperit</u>. hi filii erant Romulus et Remus. cum Amulius Rheam
9 Silviam rogavisset, quis esset pater duorum puerorum, illa respondit,
10 'Mars.'

Names

Numitor, -oris m.	Numitor
Amulius, -i m.	Amulius
Alba Longa, Albae Longae f.	Alba Longa (a city near Rome)
Rhea Silvia, Rheae Silviae f.	Rhea Silvia
Virgo Vestalis, Virginis Vestalis f.	Vestal Virgin (priestess of the goddess Vesta)
Romulus, -i m.	Romulus
Remus, -i m.	Remus
Mars, -tis m.	Mars (God of War)

Vocabulary

senior, -ius	elder	*pario, -ere, peperi*	I give birth to
expello, -ere, -puli	I drive out	*aemulus, -i* m.	rival
cogo, -ere, coegi	I force	*removeo, -ere*	I remove

1 *Numitor ... Albae Longae* (line 1): how were Numitor and Amulius
   related?   [1]

2 *post ... esse* (lines 1-2):
   (i)   what happened to the old king?   [1]
   (ii) what did Numitor expect to happen next?   [1]
   (iii) why was this?   [1]

3 *Amulius ... esset* (lines 3-4): Amulius is described as *crudelis*. What did
   he do to deserve this description?   [2]

4 *deinde ... pareret* (lines 4-5):
   (i)   what happened to Numitor's sons?   [2]
   (ii)   how was Rhea Silvia punished?   [2]
   (iii) why was she given this punishment?   [1]

5 *nam ... necata est* (lines 5-6):
   (i)   what punishment for a Vestal Virgin is mentioned here?   [1]
   (ii)   when would this punishment be given?   [2]

6 *quamquam ... peperit* (lines 7-8):
   (i)   what was Amulius anxious to do?   [1]
   (ii)   how did Rhea Silvia hinder Amulius' hopes?   [2]

7 *cum ... Mars* (lines 8-10): what did Amulius ask Rhea Silvia?   [3]

Amulius tries to kill Romulus and Remus, but fails.

rex iratus pueros militibus tradidit, ut eos in flumine necarent. milites tamen pueros in canistrum posuerunt; hoc magna cum cura in flumen posuerunt, deos orantes ut pueros servarent. flumen canistrum ad ripam tulit. ibi lupa pueros lacrimantes audivit. lupa pueris lac dedit. ita Romulus Remusque servati sunt. tandem pastor eos inventos ad uxorem portavit; quae eos multos annos educabat.

Vocabulary

flumen, -inis n.	river	*lupa, -ae* f.	she-wolf
canistrum, -i n.	basket	*lac, -tis* n.	milk
cura, -ae f.	care	*pastor, -oris* m.	shepherd
oro, -are	I beg	*educo, -are*	I bring up
ripa, -ae f.	bank (of a river)		

8   Translate the above passage into good English.   [20]

Section A Total [40]

83

Section B: Read the passage and answer the questions.

Romulus and Remus beat robbers at their own game.

1 Romulus et Remus, ubi iuvenes erant, saepe latrones oppugnabant,
2 ut praedam eorum caperent. omnem praedam inter pastores
3 dividebant. hoc cognito, tot alii iuvenes convenire coeperunt, ut mox
4 turba iuvenum esset, qui etiam plures latrones oppugnabant. tandem
5 latrones tam irati erant, ut insidias contra iuvenes facerent. quamquam
6 Romulus eis fortiter restitit, latrones Remum captum ad Amulium
7 traxerunt.
8 'hic iuvenis,' inquiunt latrones, 'turbam iuvenum contra agros
9 Numitoris ducebat.'
10 Amulius, qui nec latronibus nec Remo credidit, Numitori iuvenem
11 tradidit ut poenas daret.

Vocabulary

latro, -onis m.	bandit	*insidiae, -arum* f.pl.	ambush
oppugno, -are	I attack	*contra* + acc.	against
praeda, -ae f.	booty, loot	*resisto, -ere, -stiti* + dat.	I resist
pastor, -oris m.	shepherd	*ager, -ri* m.	land
divido, -ere	I divide	*poenas do, dare*	I am
coepi, -isse	I began		punished

9 *Romulus ... caperent* (lines 1-2): why did Romulus and Remus attack
the bandits when they grew up? [1]

10 *omnem ... dividebant* (lines 2-3): how did Romulus and Remus
help the shepherds? [2]

11 *hoc ... oppugnabant* (lines 3-4):
(i) when did the crowd of young men start to come together? [1]
(ii) what did the crowd of young men do? [1]

12 *tandem ... facerent* (lines 4-5):
(i) why do you think the bandits felt angry? [1]
(ii) what did they do as a result of feeling like this? [2]

13 *quamquam ... traxerunt* (lines 5-7):
(i) what did Romulus do? [1]
(ii) what happened to Remus? [2]

14 *hic ... ducebat* (lines 8-9): what did the bandits accuse Remus of
doing? [3]

84

15 *Amulius ... daret* (lines 10-11): why did Amulius hand over Remus
to Numitor?   [2]

16 For each of the two following Latin words, give **one** English word
which has been derived from the Latin word **and** give the meaning
of the English word.
plures
ducebat.   [4]

Section B Total [20]
Paper Total [60]

2 Section A: Read the passage and answer the questions.

The story continues from Test 1: Numitor realises who Remus is.

1   Remus, a <u>latronibus</u> captus, ad Numitorem ductus erat. Numitor
2   <u>cogitabat</u> <u>num</u> Remus <u>poenas dare</u> deberet. sed ubi Remum conspexit,
3   et cognovit eum fratrem habere, <u>attonitus</u> erat.
4   'quis est pater tuus?' Numitor rogavit.
5   '<u>nescio</u>,' respondit Remus. '<u>lupa</u> nos <u>infantes</u> e <u>flumine</u> servavit.
6   deinde <u>pastor</u> et uxor eius nos <u>educabant</u>.
7   duo <u>nepotes</u>, quos frater Amulius in <u>flumine</u> necare voluerat, statim in
8   animum Numitoris venerunt; iam erat laetissimus. Remus, cum
9   cognovisset quid Amulius fecisset, iratissimus erat. statim Remus cum
10 fratre ceterisque iuvenibus Amulium et amicos tam ferociter <u>oppugnavit</u>,
11 ut mox rex necaretur.

Names

Remus, -i m.   Remus
Numitor, -oris m.   Numitor
Amulius, -i m.   Amulius

Vocabulary

latro, -onis m.	bandit	*infans, -ntis* m.	baby
cogito, -are	I consider	*flumen, -inis* n.	river
num	whether	*pastor, -oris* m.	shepherd
poenas do, dare	I am punished	*educo, -are*	I bring up
attonitus, -a, -um	astonished	*nepos, -otis* m.	grandson
nescio, -ire	I don't know	*oppugno, -are, -avi*	I attack
lupa, -ae f.	she-wolf		

85

1   *Remus ... erat* (line 1): what **two** things had happened to Remus?   [2]

2   *Numitor ... deberet* (lines 1-2): what did Numitor consider doing?   [1]

3   *sed ... erat* (lines 2-3): what **two** things surprised Numitor?   [3]

4   *quis ... rogavit* (line 4): what question did Numitor ask?   [1]

5   *lupa ... educabant* (lines 5-6): describe the boys' childhood.   [4]

6   *duo ... laetissimus* (lines 7-8):
    (i)   what image came into Numitor's mind?   [1]
    (ii)   what should have happened to the boys?   [1]
    (iii) why do you think Numitor felt *laetissimus*?   [1]

7   *Remus ... erat* (lines 8-9): what made Remus very angry?   [2]

8   *statim ... necaretur* (lines 9-11):
    (i)   who attacked Amulius and his friends?   [3]
    (ii)   what was the result of the attack?   [1]

Romulus and Remus avenge Numitor and then set out to found a new city for themselves.

cives, ubi Romulus Remusque Numitorem regem salutaverunt, plauserunt. cum Numitor iam esset rex Albae Longae, Romulus et Remus sibi novam urbem aedificare volebant, prope locum in quo inventi erant. sed difficile erat fratribus constituere uter dux esse deberet. deos igitur oraverunt ut sibi signum darent. signo a deis ad Romulum misso, Romulus a civibus rex salutatus est.

Names

Romulus, -i m.	Romulus
Numitor, -oris m.	Numitor
Alba Longa, Albae Longae f.	Alba Longa (a city)

Vocabulary

plaudo, -ere, -si	I clap, applaud		*oro, -are, -avi*	I beg
uter, -ra, -rum	which one		*signum, -i* n.	sign
dux, -cis m.	leader			

9 Translate the above passage into good English.   [20]

Section A Total [40]

Section B: Read the passage and answer the questions.

Romulus and Remus quarrel, with fatal results.

1 Remus non erat laetus, quod frater, non ipse, a civibus novae urbis
2 iam dux lectus erat. hoc accipere nolebat. ubi <u>muros</u> urbis conspexit,
3 quos Romulus et amici eius aedificabant, eos <u>sprevit</u>.
4   'ecce!' clamavit Remus, 'hi <u>muri</u> sunt minimi: ego facile possum eos
5 <u>transilire</u>.'
6   Romulus tam iratus erat, cum fratrem <u>muros</u> <u>transilientem</u> vidisset, ut
7 eum statim necaret. ita Romulus solus <u>imperium</u> habebat. cives urbi
8 novae nomen 'Romam' dederunt, quod fideles Romulo erant. paucis
9 annis haec urbs <u>potentior</u> erat omnibus aliis urbibus.

Vocabulary

murus, -i m.	wall	*imperium, -i* n.	power
sperno, -ere, sprevi	I mock, laugh at	*potens, -ntis*	powerful
transilio, -ire	I jump over		

10 *Remus ... erat* (lines 1-2): why was Remus unhappy?   [4]

11 *hoc accipere nolebat* (line 2): what did Remus refuse to do?   [1]

12 *ubi ... sprevit* (lines 2-3): what are we told about the walls?   [2]

13 *ecce ... transilire* (lines 4-5):
    (i)   how did Remus describe the walls?   [1]
    (ii) how else did he mock the walls?   [2]

14 *Romulus ... necaret* (lines 6-7):
    (i)   why did Romulus feel angry?   [2]
    (ii) what did he do as a result?   [1]

15 *cives ... erant* (lines 7-8): why did the citizens call their new city
    Rome?   [2]

16 *paucis ... urbibus* (lines 8-9): how was Rome different from all other
    cities?   [1]

17 For each of the two following Latin words, give **one** English word
which has been derived from the Latin word **and** give the meaning
of the English word.
civibus
solus.   [4]

Section B Total [20]
Paper Total [60]

3 **Section A:**   Read the passages and answer the questions.

*Romulus' new city, called Rome, lacks citizens, and so he attracts
young men from the surrounding lands.*

1 Romulus erat rex novae urbis. Romulus, quamquam multos amicos
2 secum habebat, plures cives petere cupiebat. in urbe igitur <u>asylum</u>
3 <u>aperuit</u>. multi homines ab urbibus <u>finitimis</u> ad <u>asylum</u> mox fugiebant.
4 horum hominum multi erant servi, qui a dominis effugerant; alii <u>scelesti</u>
5 erant, qui pecunia ablata <u>aut</u> hominibus necatis fugiebant. Romulus
6 omnes <u>libenter</u> accipiebat. sed erant nullae feminae. Romulus consilium
7 quaesivit, quomodo feminis persuadere posset, ut ad urbem venirent.
8 tandem nuntios ad omnes urbes <u>finitimas</u> misit, ut cives Romam ad
9 magnum <u>spectaculum</u> invitarent. plurimae <u>familiae</u> a multis urbibus
10 Romam iter fecerunt, non solum ut <u>spectaculum</u> sed etiam ut novam
11 urbem viderent.

Names

Romulus, -i m.   Romulus

Vocabulary

asylum, -i n.	refuge, safe area	*aut*	or
aperio, -ire, -ui	I open	*libenter*	willingly
finitimus, -a, -um	neighbouring	*spectaculum, -i* n.	show, games
scelestus, -a, -um	wicked	*familia, -ae* f.	family

1 *Romulus ... urbis* (line 1): how is Romulus described?   [2]

2 *Romulus, quamquam ... cupiebat* (lines 1-2):
   (i)   whom did Romulus have with him?   [2]
   (ii) what did he want to do?   [2]

3   *multi ... fugiebant* (line 3): explain how the new city gained more citizens. [3]

4   *horum ... fugiebant* (lines 4-5): give full details of the two groups of people who came to the city. [3]

5   *sed ... feminae* (line 6): what problem was there? [1]

6   *Romulus consilium ... venirent* (lines 6-7): what was the plan Romulus was looking for? [3]

7   *tandem ... invitarent* (lines 8-9): why did Romulus send out messengers to neighbouring cities? [1]

8   *plurimae ... viderent* (lines 9-11):
    (i)   what did very many families do? [1]
    (ii) what were their **two** reasons for doing this? [2]

Romulus now solves the problem of the shortage of women.

hospites in   villas   Romanorum laete accepti sunt. novo foro et omnibus templis conspectis, attoniti erant cum cognovissent urbem tam celeriter aedificatam esse. ubi omnes parati erant spectaculum spectare, Romulus signum dedit. subito iuvenes Romani ad hospites cucurrerunt. omnes virgines, quae cum parentibus Romam venerant, raptas ad villas suas portaverunt. parentes earum, qui nulla arma secum habebant, discesserunt tristissimi.

Vocabulary

hospes, -itis m.	visitor	*virgo, -inis* f.	young woman
attonitus, -a, -um	astonished	*parens, -ntis* m.	parent
spectaculum, -i n.	show, games	*rapio, -ere, -ui, raptus*	I seize
signum, -i n.	sign	*arma, -orum* n.pl.	weapons

9   Translate the above passage into good English. [20]

Section A Total [40]

89

Section B: Read the passage and answer the questions.

Peace is finally achieved.

1 <u>parentes</u>, quorum filias Romani abstulerant, tam irati erant ut <u>ducibus</u>
2 urbium suarum persuaderent, ut Romam <u>oppugnarent</u>. Romani tamen
3 eos facile vicerunt. novae uxores Romanorum, quamquam iuvenes eas
4 tam crudeliter ceperant, iam laetiores erant, quod <u>mariti</u> eis amorem et
5 dona et pulchras villas dederant. feminae igitur, postquam <u>parentes</u>
6 cum maiore <u>exercitu</u> redierunt, in medium <u>proelium</u> cucurrerunt, patres
7 <u>maritosque</u> <u>orantes</u> ut pacem facerent.
8 'nos,' inquiunt, 'sumus <u>causa</u> <u>belli</u>. in nos <u>iram</u> <u>gladiosque</u> <u>vertite</u>.
9 melius est nobis perire quam <u>sine</u> <u>maritis</u>, <u>sine</u> patribus vivere.'
10 <u>duces</u>, postquam hoc audiverunt, pacem fecerunt.

Vocabulary

parens, -ntis m.	parent	*causa, -ae* f.	cause
dux, -cis m.	leader	*bellum, -i* n.	war
oppugno, -are	I attack	*ira, -ae* f.	anger
maritus, -i m.	husband	*gladius, -i* m.	sword
exercitus, -us m.	army	*verto, -ere*	I turn
proelium, -i n.	battle	*sine* + abl.	without
oro, -are	I beg		

10 *parentes ... oppugnarent* (lines 1-2):
   (i)   what had happened to the daughters?   [1]
   (ii) what did the parents do as a result of their anger?   [2]

11 *Romani ... vicerunt* (lines 2-3): what happened in this first battle?   [2]

12 *novae ... dederant* (lines 3-5):
   (i)   how did the new wives of the Romans feel?   [1]
   (ii) what was surprising about the fact that they felt this way?   [1]
   (iii) why did they feel this way?   [3]

13 *feminae ... facerent* (lines 5-7):
   (i)   when the parents of the women returned, what was different
       about their army?   [1]
   (ii) what did the women do when they ran into the middle of the
       battle?   [1]

14 *nos ... vertite* (line 8): what did the women tell the men to do?   [2]

15 *melius ... vivere* (line 9): what is the women's argument here?   [2]

16 For each of the two following Latin words, give **one** English word
which has been derived from the Latin word **and** give the meaning
of the English word.
urbium
novae. [4]

Section B Total [20]
Paper Total [60]

4 Section A: Read the passages and answer the questions.

The Etruscans, thrown out of Rome, seek the help of Lars Porsenna.

1 Lars Porsenna erat rex Clusii. haec urbs, quam Etrusci multis annis
2 <u>antea</u> aedificaverant, iam magnum <u>imperium</u> habebat. Porsenna ipse
3 erat Etruscus. ubi Romani, post longum <u>bellum</u>, regem suum,
4 Tarquinium, <u>expulerunt</u>, ille, quod erat Etruscus, ad Porsennam
5 festinavit, ut auxilium eius peteret.
6 'ego,' inquit, 'sum Etruscus; tu quoque es Etruscus. nos <u>una</u>
7 pugnare debemus.'
8 Porsenna, qui <u>imperium</u> <u>crescens</u> Romae timebat, statim <u>consensit</u>.
9 magnum <u>exercitum</u> igitur in <u>agros</u> Romanorum duxit. omnes cives
10 Romani ex <u>agris</u> in urbem fugerunt. Porsenna, quamquam urbem
11 vehementer <u>oppugnavit</u>, intrare non poterat, quod pars urbis <u>muris</u>, pars
12 <u>flumine</u> muniebatur.

Names

Lars Porsenna, Lartis Porsennae m.	Lars Porsenna
Clusium, -i n.	Clusium (a city near Rome)
Etrusci, -orum m.pl.	the Etruscans (a race of people who lived in central Italy)
Etruscus, -a, -um	Etruscan
Tarquinius, -i m.	Tarquinius (the last king of Rome)

Vocabulary

antea	before	*cresco, -ere*	I grow
imperium, -i n.	power	*consentio, -ire, -sensi*	I agree
bellum, -i n.	war	*exercitus, -us* m.	army
expello, -ere, -puli	I drive out	*agri, -orum* m.pl.	territory, land
una	together	*oppugno, -are, -avi*	I attack

| *murus, -i* m. | wall | *munio, -ire* | I defend |
| *flumen, -inis* n. | river | | |

1   *Lars ...Clusii* (line 1): who was Lars Porsenna?   [1]

2   *haec ... habebat* (lines 1-2):
    (i)   what are we told about the previous history of Clusium?   [3]
    (ii)   what was it like now?   [1]

3   *ubi ... peteret* (lines 3-5):
    (i)   what happened in Rome?   [2]
    (ii)   what was the purpose of Tarquinius' visit to Porsenna?   [2]
    (iii)   why did Tarquinius choose Porsenna in particular?   [1]

4   *ego ... debemus* (lines 6-7):
    (i)   what does Tarquinius think they should do?   [1]
    (ii)   what reason does he give for this?   [1]

5   *Porsenna ... consensit* (line 8): why was Porsenna ready to do
as he was asked?   [2]

6   *magnum ... fugerunt* (lines 9-10):
    (i)   what did Porsenna do?   [2]
    (ii)   what did this cause the Roman citizens to do?   [1]

7   *Porsenna ... muniebatur* (lines 10-12):
    (i)   what could Porsenna not do?   [1]
    (ii)   why was this?   [2]

Porsenna attacks Rome but the only way in is defended by Horatius, a Roman soldier.

sed <u>pons</u> erat, qui <u>hostibus</u> viam ad mediam urbem dare poterat. pauci milites Romani hunc <u>pontem</u> custodiebant sed, <u>hostibus</u> conspectis, fugere volebant. Horatius tamen eis persuasit ut manerent.
    'si vultis,' inquit, 'hostibus urbem tradere, fugite; si tamen <u>libertatem</u> cupitis, mecum manete <u>pontemque</u> delete.'
    Romani, his <u>verbis</u> victi, <u>pontem</u> delere <u>coeperunt</u>. <u>interea</u> Horatius in <u>ponte</u> solus stabat, <u>hostes</u> exspectans.

Name

Horatius, -i m.   Horatius

Vocabulary

pons, -tis m.	bridge	*verbum, -i* n.	word
hostes, -ium m.pl.	the enemy	*coepi, -isse*	I began
libertas, -atis f.	freedom	*interea*	meanwhile

8   Translate the above passage into good English.   [20]

Section A Total [40]

Section B: Read the passage and answer the questions.

Peace is finally achieved.

1   Horatius hostibus diu resistebat; tandem, ponte deleto, in flumen
2   desiluit. Porsenna, cum urbem intrare non posset, nunc eam obsidere
3   coepit. multos post dies iuvenis Romanus, Mucius nomine, Porsennam
4   necare constituit. regi amicisque clam appropinquavit sed, cum regem
5   non cognovisset, non illum sed scribam eius necavit. Porsenna milites
6   iuvenem captum necare iussit.
7   'me necare potes,' clamavit Mucius, 'sed erunt multi alii iuvenes
8   Romani, qui te necare volunt. necesse est tibi semper cavere.'
9   hoc audito, Porsenna tam perterritus erat, ut milites suos ab urbe
10 statim duceret. tandem cives intellexerunt se servatos esse.

Names

Mucius, -i m.   Mucius

Vocabulary

hostes, -ium m.pl.	the enemy	*coepi, -isse*	I began
resisto, -ere + dat.	I resist	*dies, -ei* m.	day
pons, -tis m.	bridge	*clam*	furtively
flumen, -inis n.	river	*scriba, -ae* m.	secretary
desilio, -ire, -ui	I jump down	*necesse*	necessary
obsideo, -ere	I besiege, blockade	*caveo, -ere*	I watch out

9   *Horatius ... desiluit* (lines 1-2):
    (i)   what did Horatius do after resisting the enemy?   [1]
    (ii) when did he do this?   [1]

93

10 *Porsenna ... coepit* (lines 2-3): why did Porsenna start to besiege
the city?   [1]

11 *multos ... constituit* (lines 3-4):
(i)   what did Mucius decide to do?   [1]
(ii) when did he do this?   [1]

12 *regi ... necavit* (lines 4-5): describe fully how and why Mucius' plan
went wrong.   [4]

13 *Porsenna ... iussit* (lines 5-6): what did Porsenna do?   [3]

14 *me ... cavere* (lines 7-8): what threat did Mucius make?   [2]

15 *hoc ... esse* (lines 9-10):
(i)   what did Porsenna's fear lead him to do?   [1]
(ii) what did the Roman citizens realise?   [1]

16 For each of the two following Latin words, give **one** English word
which has been derived from the Latin word **and** give the meaning
of the English word.
regi
intellexerunt.   [4]

Section B Total [20]
Paper Total [60]

5 **Section A:**   Read the passages and answer the questions.

King Aegeus falls in love with the daughter of a friend.

1 Aegeus erat rex Athenarum. Aegeus, quamquam uxorem habebat,
2 nec filios nec filias habebat. cum filium habere <u>valde</u> cuperet, per
3 Graeciam iter faciebat, ut consilium amicorum peteret. ad urbem venit,
4 in qua amicus eius, Pittheus nomine, erat rex. Pittheus, quem Aegeus
5 diu non <u>visitaverat</u>, filiam pulcherrimam habebat, Aethram nomine. ubi
6 Aegeus Aethram conspexit, eam statim amavit. postquam unam
7 noctem amori dederunt, Aegeus tristis erat. dixit se Aethram amare:
8 'quamquam,' inquit, 'ego te amo, <u>necesse</u> est mihi Athenas redire; nam
9 ibi uxor me exspectat.' Aethra tristis erat, quod Aegeus discedere
10 constituerat. Aegeus, <u>antequam</u> Aethram reliquit, eam <u>oravit</u> ut filium
11 sibi daret; deinde abiit.

Names

Aegeus, -i m.	Aegeus	*Athenae, -arum* f.pl.	Athens
Graecia, -ae f.	Greece	*Pittheus, -i* m.	Pittheus
Aethra, -ae f.	Aethra		

Vocabulary

valde	very much	*antequam*	before
visito, -are, -avi	I visit	*oro, -are, -avi*	I beg
necesse	necessary		

1   Who was Aegeus (line 1)? [1]

2   *Aegeus, quamquam ... filias habebat* (lines 1-2):
   (i)   what did Aegeus have? [1]
   (ii) what did he not have? [2]

3   *cum ... peteret* (lines 2-3):
   (i)   what was Aegeus' great wish? [1]
   (ii) why did he travel through Greece? [2]

4   *ad urbem ... nomine* (lines 3-5): give **three** details about Pittheus. [3]

5   *ubi ... amavit* (lines 5-6): what happened when Aegeus saw Aethra? [1]

6   *postquam ... amare* (lines 6-7):
   (i)   how long did Aegeus and Aethra spend together? [1]
   (ii)   how did Aegeus feel after this period of time? [1]
   (iii) why do you think he felt like this? [1]
   (iv)   what did he tell Aethra? [1]

7   *quamquam ... exspectat* (lines 8-9):
   (i)   what did Aegeus have to do? [1]
   (ii) why was this? [2]

8   *Aethra ... constituerat* (lines 9-10): why was Aethra *tristis*? [1]

9   *Aegeus, antequam ... abiit* (lines 10-11): what did Aegeus beg Aethra to do before he left? [1]

95

Theseus grows up.

Aethra filium <u>peperit</u>. puero nomen Theseum dedit. paucis annis Theseus <u>sapientior</u> fortiorque erat quam omnes alii pueri. ubi Theseus iuvenis erat, mater ei, 'in silvam festina,' inquit; 'ibi magnum <u>saxum</u> videbis. sub <u>saxo</u> <u>gladium</u> invenies, quem pater tuus <u>celavit</u>. fer mihi illum <u>gladium</u>.' Theseus in silvam cucurrit, ut <u>saxum</u> peteret; quo conspecto mox <u>gladium</u> invenit.

Name

Theseus, -i m.   Theseus

Vocabulary

pario, -ere, peperi	I give birth to
sapiens, -ntis	wise
saxum, -i n.	rock
gladius, -i m.	sword
celo, -are, celavi	I hide

10 Translate the above passage into good English.   [20]

Section A Total [40]

Section B: Read the passage and answer the questions.

Aethra explains about the sword.

1 <u>gladio</u> invento, Theseus primo iratus erat, quod <u>gladius</u> <u>robiginosus</u>
2 erat; deinde, cum intellexisset patrem suum illum <u>gladium</u> olim
3 portavisse, eum ad matrem laetius tulit. illa, ubi <u>gladium</u> conspexit, filio
4 laudato, tam tristis fuit ut statim lacrimaret.
5   'hic <u>gladius</u>,' inquit Aethra, 'erat patris tui, qui eum sub <u>saxo</u> posuit.
6 <u>antequam</u> me reliquit, mihi hoc dixit: "ego te <u>oro</u>: da mihi filium; <u>postea</u>
7 eum cum hoc <u>gladio</u> ad me mitte." nunc igitur tibi <u>necesse</u> est Athenas
8 iter facere.' quamquam Theseus matrem rogavit quis pater esset, illa
9 eum iussit id rogare cum Athenas advenisset.

Vocabulary

gladius, -i m.	sword
robiginosus, -a, -um	rusty
saxum, -i n.	rock
antequam	before
oro, -are	I beg
postea	later
necesse	necessary

11 *gladio ... tulit* (lines 1-3):
   (i)   when did Theseus feel angry? [1]
   (ii) why did he feel like this? [1]
   (iii) what made Theseus feel differently? [2]
   (iv) what did he then do? [2]

12 *illa ... lacrimaret* (lines 3-4): what **two** things did Aethra do when she saw the sword? [2]

13 *hic ... posuit* (line 5): what did Aethra tell Theseus about the sword? [2]

14 *antequam ... mitte* (lines 6-7): what two commands did Aegeus give to Aethra? [3]

15 *nunc ... facere* (lines 7-8): what must Theseus now do? [1]

16 *quamquam ... advenisset* (lines 8-9):
   (i)   what did Theseus ask Aethra? [1]
   (ii) how did she reply? [1]

17 For each of the two following Latin words, give **one** English word which has been derived from the Latin word **and** give the meaning of the English word.
primo
portavisse. [4]

Section B Total [20]
Paper Total [60]

Section 5. Tests for WJEC Level 2 Core

Introduction

These are momentum tests, with each story split into three sections. The first and third of these sections are assessed by comprehension questions, while the second section is tested by translation. The range of comprehension questions is identical to that in the Level 1 Core tests, with the exception of the derivation question, which does not appear in Level 1.

The term 'momentum' indicates an increasing level of demand as the test progresses. This means that the first section should be accessible to virtually all students, because the Latin contains few linguistic hurdles and the questions are mostly straightforward. The translation section becomes harder as it progresses, while the last section contains the most complex Latin and most searching questions.

The storylines are taken from either history or mythology. The mark scheme for the translation is the same as that used for the Level 1 Additional tests.

In each exercise, read the first part of the story and answer the questions that follow. Then translate the second part of the story. Then read the final part and answer the questions that follow.

1 The story of Cronus and Rhea

1 The world is ruled by the Titans, of whom the strongest is Cronus. Cronus is afraid of an oracle that has predicted a dreadful future for him.

1 inter Titanos erat Cronus. Cronus uxorem habebat, Rheam nomine.
2 Rhea maritum et amabat et timebat; ille enim crudelis erat. ubi filia <u>nata</u>
3 <u>est</u>, Rhea laeta erat; <u>infanti</u> pulchrae nomen Vestam dedit. Cronus
4 tamen erat iratus, quod <u>oraculum</u> audiverat: '<u>liberi</u> tui,' inquit <u>oraculum</u>,
5 'te <u>necabunt</u>.' Cronus igitur consilium dirum cepit. ubi Rhea ei Vestam
6 tradidit ut eam teneret, eam statim consumpsit. quamquam Cronus iam
7 laetior erat, Rhea perterrita erat.

Names

| Titanus, -i m. | Titan | Cronus, -i m. | Cronus |
| Rhea, -ae f. | Rhea | Vesta, -ae f. | Vesta |

Words

nata est	was born
infans, -ntis m. / f.	baby
oraculum, -i n.	oracle (a prediction of the future)
liberi, -orum m.pl.	children
necabunt	will kill

(a) *inter ... Cronus* (line 1): what are we told here about Cronus? [1]

(b) Who was Rhea (line 1)? [1]

(c) *Rhea ... erat* (line 2):
  (i) what **two** feelings did Rhea have towards Cronus? [2]
  (ii) why did she have the second of these feelings? [1]

(d) *ubi ... dedit* (lines 2-3):
  (i) pick out and translate a Latin word that describes Rhea. [2]
  (ii) what caused her to be like that? [1]
  (iii) pick out and translate a Latin word that describes Vesta. [2]

(e) *Cronus ... necabunt* (lines 3-5): which **three** of the following statements are true? Write down the letters for the ones that are correct.
  A Cronus was angry
  B Cronus was happy
  C Cronus was listening to an oracle
  D Cronus had heard an oracle
  E the oracle would kill Cronus' children
  F the oracle said Cronus' children would kill him   [3]

(f) *Cronus ... cepit* (line 5): what did Cronus do?   [3]

(g) *ubi ... consumpsit* (lines 5-6):
  (i)   what did Rhea do?   [2]
  (ii)   why did she do this?   [2]
  (iii) what did Cronus do?   [2]
  (iv)   write down an English word that comes from *tradidit*.   [1]

(h) *quamquam ... erat* (lines 6-7):
  (i)   which is the correct translation of *Cronus iam laetior erat*?
         A now Cronus was happy
         B now Cronus was happier
         C now Cronus was very happy
         D now Cronus was the happiest   [1]
  (ii)   how did Rhea feel at the end?   [1]

Total mark for Question 1: [25]

2   *Rhea devises a plan to fool Cronus.*

ubi paucos post annos filius <u>natus est</u>, Cronus eum quoque consumpsit. hoc modo tres alii <u>liberi</u>, simulac <u>nati sunt</u>, perierunt. Rhea nesciebat quid facere posset; <u>liberos</u> enim cupiebat, sed nolebat eos Crono tradere. postquam filius alius tandem <u>natus est</u>, cui nomen Iovem dedit, Rhea optimum consilium cepit. primum matri et patri <u>infantem</u> dedit; deinde, cum Cronus advenisset filium postulans, ei <u>saxum</u> <u>vestibus</u> <u>involutum</u> tradidit. <u>dum</u> ei hoc dabat, tam vehementer clamabat et lacrimabat, ut Cronus <u>saxum</u> consumeret <u>ignarus</u>. postquam Cronus laetus abiit, Rhea etiam laetior ad matrem patremque festinavit, qui Iovem in <u>spelunca</u> iam celaverant. ibi eum curabant. Iuppiter, ubi <u>adultus</u> erat, Cronum <u>punire</u> constituit.

Name

Iuppiter, Iovis m.   Jupiter

Words

natus est, nati sunt	was born / were born
liberi, -orum m.pl.	children
infans, -ntis m. / f.	baby
saxum, -i n.	stone
vestes, -ium f. pl.	clothes
involvo, -ere, -vi, -utus	I wrap
dum	while
ignarus, -a, -um	without realising
spelunca, -ae f.	cave
adultus, -a, -um	grown up
punio, -ire	I punish

[40]

3   *Jupiter takes revenge on Cronus.*

1   Iuppiter, cum optimum vinum paravisset, ad Cronum ivit. Cronus, quod
2   eum numquam antea viderat, nescivit quis esset. Cronus, simulac
3   vinum <u>bibit</u>, plus vini postulavit. mox tantum vinum <u>biberat</u>, ut omnia
4   quae in <u>ventre</u> continebantur <u>evomeret</u>. omnia <u>fragmenta</u> quinque
5   <u>liberorum</u>, quos consumpserat, aderant. haec <u>fragmenta</u> convenerunt.
6   mox tres feminae duoque viri prope Iovem stabant. Cronus <u>attonitus</u>
7   fuit. 'qui vos estis?' inquit. 'nos sumus tui <u>liberi</u>,' illi responderunt. 'te
8   punire volumus, quod nos necavisti.' in bello quod gesserunt, Iuppiter et
9   fratres et <u>sorores</u> patrem superaverunt. deinde Iuppiter rex deorum erat.

Words

bibo, -ere, bibi	I drink
venter, ventris m.	stomach
evomo, -ere	I vomit up, spew out
fragmentum, -i n.	fragment, piece
liberi, -orum m.pl.	children
attonitus, -a, -um	astonished
soror, -oris f.	sister

(a) *Iuppiter ... ivit* (line 1): which **three** of the following statements are true? Write down the letters for the ones that are correct.
  A Jupiter was very good
  B Jupiter prepared some wine
  C the wine was very good
  D some very good wine appeared
  E Jupiter went to Cronus
  F Cronus went to Jupiter   [3]

(b) *Cronus ... esset* (lines 1-2):
  (i)   what did Cronus not know?   [2]
  (ii) why was this?   [3]

(c) *Cronus ... postulavit* (lines 2-3): what did the wine cause Cronus to do?   [2]

(d) *mox ... evomeret* (lines 3-4):
  (i)   which is the correct translation of *mox tantum vinum biberat*?
        A soon he was drinking so much wine
        B soon he drank so much wine
        C soon he had drunk so much wine
        D soon so much wine was drunk   [1]
  (ii) what did Cronus vomit up?   [3]

(e) *omnia ... aderant* (lines 4-5): which **three** of the following statements are true? Write down the letters for the ones that are correct.
  A there were five children
  B there were five pieces of children
  C the children had eaten the pieces
  D Cronus had eaten the children
  E all the pieces were present
  F Cronus and Rhea were present   [3]

(f) Which is the correct translation of *haec fragmenta convenerunt* (line 5)?
  A this was a convenient piece
  B the pieces came together here
  C these pieces came together
  D these were convenient pieces   [1]

(g) *mox ... stabant* (line 6): what soon happened?   [6]

(h) *qui ... responderunt* (line 7):
  (i)   what did Cronus ask?   [2]
  (ii) what reply was he given?   [2]

(i) *te ... necavisti* (lines 7-8):
   (i) what did the speakers want to do? [1]
   (ii) what reason did they give for this? [2]

(j) *in bello ... superaverunt* (lines 8-9):
   (i) which is the correct translation of *in bello quod gesserunt*?
   - A because they were fighting a war
   - B because they fought in a war
   - C they fought in this war
   - D in the war which they fought [1]
   (ii) write down the Latin word that tells us who was defeated. [1]

(k) *deinde ... erat* (line 9): what did Jupiter become? [2]

Total mark for Question 3: [35]

2   Aeneas arrives at Carthage

1   *At the end of the Trojan War, Aeneas, who is a member of the royal*
    family of Troy, gathers together the Trojan survivors and sails away to
    establish a new home. They are blown off course.

1   Aeneas erat princeps Troianus. Aeneas, postquam Graeci urbem
2   eius deleverunt, cum patre et filio et omnibus aliis, quos Graeci non
3   necaverant, ab urbe fugerat. iam omnes trans mare navigabant, ut
4   novam urbem <u>conderent</u>. sed <u>tempestas</u> ingens naves ad Africam
5   <u>pepulit</u>. cum navis in qua Aeneas navigabat ad terram advenisset,
6   Aeneas laetissimus erat quod pater et filius etiam vivebant. ceteras
7   naves tamen conspicere non poterat. Aeneas ad summum <u>collem</u>
8   ambulavit, ut <u>circumspectaret</u>.

Names

Aeneas, -ae m.	Aeneas	*Troianus, -a, -um*	Trojan
Graeci, -orum m.pl.	the Greeks	*Africa, -ae* f.	Africa

Words

condo, -ere	I found, build
tempestas, -atis f.	storm
pello,-ere, pepuli	I drive
collis, -is m.	hill
circumspecto, -are	I look round

(a) Which is the best translation of *Aeneas erat princeps Troianus* (line 1)?
    A Aeneas was a Trojan principal
    B Aeneas was a Trojan chieftain
    C Aeneas was a Trojan emperor
    D Aeneas was previously a Trojan   [1]

(b) *Aeneas, postquam ... fugerat* (lines 1-3):
    (i)   what happened to Troy?   [2]
    (ii) what **two** members of his family accompanied Aeneas?   [2]
    (iii) which other people accompanied him?   [3]
    (iv) which is the correct translation of *ab urbe fugerat*?
        A they had fled from the city
        B he fled from the city
        C they fled from the city
        D he had fled from the city   [1]

(c) *iam ... conderent* (lines 3-4): which **two** of the following statements are true? Write down the letters for the ones that are correct.
    A they were all crossing the sea
    B they were crossing all the seas
    C they were building a new city
    D they wanted to build a new city   [2]

(d) *sed ... pepulit* (lines 4-5): how did their plans go wrong?   [3]

(e) *cum ... vivebant* (lines 5-6):
    (i)   which ship reached land?   [1]
    (ii) write down and translate the Latin word that tells us how Aeneas felt.   [2]
    (iii) why did he feel like this?   [3]

(f) *ceteras ... poterat* (lines 6-7): how do you think this would have made Aeneas feel? Give a reason for your answer.   [2]

(g) *Aeneas ... circumspectaret* (lines 7-8):
    (i)   what did Aeneas do?   [2]
    (ii) why did he do this?   [1]

Total mark for Question 1: [25]

2   *Aeneas meets a girl, who tells him about the land and its people.*

Aeneas terram, ad quam venerat, spectare volebat. auxilium enim
petere cupiebat, sed neque urbem neque homines videre poterat. cum
ibi staret, puella pulcherrima ei appropinquavit. Aeneas, postquam
puellam salutavit, eam rogavit num ab urbe propinqua venisset.
     puella, 'ita vero,' respondit. 'nomen urbis est Carthago. Carthago est
nova urbs, quam regina Dido celeriter aedificat. Dido cum multis civibus
a patria fugit, quod frater eam necare cupiebat, ut ipse imperium
teneret. sed quis es tu?'
     Aeneas puellae totam rem libenter narravit. deinde puella, in
formam deae mutata, subito eum reliquit: puella enim erat Venus, mater
Aeneae. Aeneas iratus erat, quod mater eum ita deceperat.

Names

Carthago, -inis f.   Carthage   Dido, -onis f.   Dido
Venus, -eris f.   Venus

Words

propinquus, -a, -um   nearby
ita vero   yes
regina, -ae f.   queen
patria, -ae f.   homeland
forma, -ae f.   appearance
muto, -are, -avi, -atus   I change
decipio, -ere, decepi   I deceive

                                                              [40]

3   *Queen Dido welcomes Aeneas and his people.*

1   cum Aeneas ad suos rediisset, ipse et pauci amici ad urbem Didonis
2   festinaverunt. ubi urbi appropinquabant, multos homines viderunt
3   templa, forum et domos aedificantes. in medio stabat Dido, femina
4   pulcherrima. regina tam attonita fuit, cum Aeneam et amicos
5   conspexisset, ut primo nesciret quid dicere deberet. simulac tamen
6   Aeneas reginae nomen suum dixit, laetissima erat. 'magnus,' inquit,
7   'honor est nobis vos excipere. nos enim multa de bello Troiano et virtute
8   Aeneae audivimus. cenam optimam vobis parare debemus.' Aeneas
9   ceteros suos a nave arcessivit, gaudens quod in periculum non
10 advenerant.

106

Words

attonitus, -a, -um	astonished
honor, -oris m.	honour
excipio, -ere	I welcome
virtus, -utis f.	courage
arcesso, -ere, -ivi	I summon

(a) Which is the correct translation of *cum* (line 1)?
    A with
    B since
    C although
    D when   [1]

(b) *ipse ... festinaverunt* (lines 1-2):
    (i)   who travelled to the city?   [3]
    (ii) write down and translate the Latin word that gives information
         about the city.   [2]

(c) *ubi ... aedificantes* (lines 2-3):
    (i)   when did they see many men?   [2]
    (ii) what were the men doing?   [4]
    (iii) write down an English word that comes from *multos*.   [1]

(d) *in medio ... pulcherrima* (lines 3-4):
    (i)   where was Dido standing?   [1]
    (ii) how is she described?   [2]

(e) *regina ... deberet* (lines 4-5): which **three** of the following statements
are true? Write down the letters for the ones that are correct.
    A Aeneas was astonished
    B Dido was astonished
    C the queen saw Aeneas and his friends
    D Aeneas saw his friends
    E Aeneas did not know what to say
    F Dido did not know what to say   [3]

(f) *simulac ... erat* (lines 5-6):
    (i)   which person in this sentence is described as *laetissima*?   [1]
    (ii) what caused this person to feel like this?   [3]

(g) Which is the correct translation of *magnus honor est nobis vos excipere* (lines 6-7)?

      A it is great for us to welcome you with honour
      B it is a great honour for us to welcome you
      C it is a great honour for you to welcome us
      D we welcomed you with great honour   [1]

(h) *nos ... debemus* (lines 7-8):
      (i) what have the people of Carthage heard?   [4]
      (ii) what must they now do?   [4]

(i) *Aeneas ... advenerant* (lines 8-10): which **three** of the following statements are true? Write down the letters for the ones that are correct.

      A Aeneas summoned the rest of his men
      B Aeneas looked for the rest of his ships
      C the men rejoiced
      D Aeneas rejoiced
      E they were safe
      F they were not safe   [3]

Total mark for Question 3: [35]

3   *The story of Theseus (1)*

1   *King Aegeus falls in love with the daughter of a friend.*

1 Aegeus erat rex Athenarum. Aegeus, quamquam uxorem habebat,
2 nec filios nec filias habebat. quod filium habere <u>valde</u> cupiebat, per
3 Graeciam iter faciebat, ut consilium amicorum peteret. ad urbem venit,
4 in qua amicus eius, Pittheus nomine, erat rex. Pittheus, quem Aegeus
5 diu non <u>visitaverat</u>, filiam pulcherrimam habebat. haec filia erat Aethra.
6 simulatque Aegeus Aethram conspexit, eam amavit. postquam unam
7 noctem amori dederunt, Aegeus tristis erat. Aethrae dixit: 'quamquam
8 ego te amo, <u>necesse</u> est mihi Athenas redire; ibi enim uxor me
9 exspectat.'

Names

Aegeus, -i m.	Aegeus	*Athenae, -arum* f.pl.	Athens
Graecia, -ae f.	Greece	*Pittheus, -i* m.	Pittheus
Aethra, -ae f.	Aethra		

Words

valde	very much
visito, -are, -avi	I visit
necesse	necessary

(a) Who was Aegeus (line 1)? [1]

(b) *Aegeus, quamquam ... habebat* (lines 1-2):
    (i)   what did Aegeus have? [1]
    (ii) what did he not have? [2]

(c) *quod ... peteret* (lines 2-3):
    (i)   what was Aegeus' great wish? [2]
    (ii) why did he travel through Greece? [3]

(d) *ad urbem ... rex* (lines 3-4): which **three** of the following statements are true? Write down the letters for the ones that are correct.
    A Aegeus came to a city
    B Pittheus came to a city
    C a friend of Aegeus lived in the city
    D Aegeus was the king of this city
    E Pittheus was the name of the city
    F Pittheus was the name of the king of the city [3]

(e) *Pittheus ... habebat* (lines 4-5):
    (i)   write down and translate the Latin word that tells us how long it was since Aegeus saw Pittheus. [2]
    (ii) what are we told about Pittheus' family? [2]

(f) Which is the correct translation of *haec filia erat Aethra* (line 5)?
    A this was the daughter of Aethra
    B Aethra's daughter was here
    C this daughter was Aethra
    D Aethra was the daughter of this man [1]

(g) *simulatque ... amavit* (line 6): what happened when Aegeus saw Aethra? [2]

(h) *postquam ... erat* (lines 6-7):
    (i)   write down and translate the Latin words that tell us how long Aegeus and Aethra spent together. [2]
    (ii) how did Aegeus feel after this period of time? [1]

(i) *quamquam ... exspectat* (lines 7-9):
  (i)   what did Aegeus have to do?   [1]
  (ii) why was this?   [2]

Total mark for Question 1: [25]

2   *Aethra gives birth to a son.*

Aethra tristis erat, quod Aegeus discedere constituerat. Aegeus, <u>antequam</u> Aethram reliquit, eam oravit ut filium sibi daret; deinde abiit. novem post <u>mensibus</u> Aethra filium <u>peperit</u>. puero nomen Theseum dedit. Aethra ipsa Theseum tam bene docebat, ut mox <u>sapientior</u> fortiorque esset quam omnes alii pueri.

ubi Theseus iuvenis erat, mater ei, 'in silvam festina,' inquit. 'nam in media silva est magnum <u>saxum</u>. sub <u>saxo</u> iacet gladius, quem pater tuus celavit. fer mihi illum gladium.'

Theseus in silvam cucurrit, ut <u>saxum</u> quaereret; quod mox conspexit. primo <u>saxum</u>, quamquam <u>trusit</u>, <u>movere</u> non poterat. circum <u>saxum</u> ambulavit, id spectans iratus. deinde ab una sola <u>parte</u> <u>saxum</u> <u>movere</u> potuit.

Names

Theseus, -i m.   Theseus

Words

antequam	before
mensis, -is m.	month
pario, -ere, peperi	I give birth to
sapiens, -ntis	sensible
saxum, -i n.	rock
trudo, -ere, -si	I push
moveo, -ere	I move
pars, -tis f.	(here) direction

[40]

3   *Theseus finds the sword.*

1   tandem Theseus <u>saxum</u> <u>movit</u>. ibi sub <u>saxo</u> iacebat gladius, ab eo
2   quaesitus. primo Theseus iratus erat, quod gladius <u>robiginosus</u> erat;
3   deinde, cum pater gladium olim gessisset, eum ad matrem laete tulit.
4   mater Thesei, simulac conspexit gladium, tam tristis fuit ut statim
5   lacrimaret.
6   'hic gladius,' inquit, 'erat patris tui, qui eum sub <u>saxo</u> celavit.
7   <u>antequam</u> me reliquit, mihi haec verba dixit: "ego te oro: da mihi filium;
8   postea eum cum hoc gladio ad me mitte." nunc igitur tibi <u>necesse</u> est
9   Athenas iter facere.'

Words

saxum, -i n.	rock
moveo, -ere	I move
robiginosus, -a, -um	rusty
antequam	before
necesse	necessary

(a) What did Theseus do at last?   [1]

(b) *ibi ... quaesitus* (lines 1-2):
   (i)   where was the sword?   [1]
   (ii) how is the sword described?   [2]

(c) *primo ... tulit* (lines 2-3):
   (i)   write down and translate the Latin word in line 2 that tells us how
      Theseus felt.   [2]
   (ii) why did he feel like this?   [2]
   (iii) which Latin word in this sentence does a similar job to *primo*?   [1]
   (iv) what made Theseus feel differently?   [3]
   (v)   what did he then do?   [3]

(d) *mater ... lacrimaret* (lines 4-5): which **three** of the following statements
are true? Write down the letters for the ones that are correct.
   A   Theseus saw the sword
   B   Theseus' mother saw the sword
   C   Theseus' mother was sad
   D   Theseus was sad
   E   Theseus burst into tears
   F   Theseus' mother burst into tears   [3]

(e) *hic ... celavit* (line 6):
  (i)   write down an English word that comes from *patris*.   [1]
  (ii) which is the correct translation of *hic gladius erat patris tui*?
        A here was your father's sword
        B your father was given this sword
        C your father was a gladiator
        D this sword belonged to your father   [1]
  (iii) what did Theseus' father do?   [3]

(f) *antequam ... dixit* (line 7): write down the names of the following people:
  (i)   the person who *me reliquit*   [1]
  (ii) the person who *haec verba dixit*   [1]
  (iii) the person to whom *haec verba* were spoken   [1]

(g) *ego ... mitte* (lines 7-8):
  (i)   what did the speaker want?   [2]
  (ii) what was the second command he gave (*postea ... mitte*)?   [5]

(h) *nunc ... facere* (lines 8-9): what must Theseus now do?   [2]

Total mark for Question 3: [35]

4 The story of Theseus (2)

1 Aethra tells Theseus to go to Athens.

1 Theseus erat filius Aethrae. Theseus, ubi iuvenis erat, gladium
2 patris invenit. deinde Aethra eum Athenas ire iussit.
3   'iam tibi discedendum est,' Aethra inquit. 'sed iter longum
4 periculosissimumque est, quod multi latrones viatores oppugnant.
5 melius est tibi in nave ire.'
6   Theseus cognoscere volebat, quis esset pater; mater enim ei
7 nomen patris numquam dixerat. mater tamen hoc dicere noluit.
8   'ad regiam i,' inquit. 'regi illum gladium ostende. deinde rex ipse tibi
9 omnia dicere potest, quae cognoscere vis.'

Names

| Theseus, -i m. | Theseus | Aethra, -ae f. | Aethra |
| Athenae, -arum f.pl. | Athens | | |

112

Words

periculosus, -a, -um	dangerous
latro, -onis m.	robber, bandit
viator, -oris m.	traveller
regia, -ae f.	palace

(a) Who was Theseus (line 1)? [2]

(b) *Theseus ... invenit* (lines 1-2):
  (i) what did Theseus find? [2]
  (ii) write down and translate the Latin word that tells us how old
       Theseus was at the time. [2]

(c) *deinde ... iussit* (line 2): what did Aethra do? [3]

(d) Which is the correct translation of *iam tibi discedendum est* (line 3)?
  A now you are departing
  B now I am departing to see you
  C now you must depart
  D now you have departed [1]

(e) *sed ... oppugnant* (lines 3-4):
  (i) how does Aethra describe the journey by land? [2]
  (ii) what reason does she give for describing it like this? [3]

(f) *melius ... ire* (line 5): what method of travel does Aethra
    recommend? [1]

(g) *Theseus ... noluit* (lines 6-7): which **three** of the following statements
    are true? Write down the letters for the ones that are correct.
  A Theseus wanted to find out who his father was
  B Theseus was wanting to understand his father
  C Aethra had never told Theseus' father his name
  D Aethra had never told Theseus the name of his father
  E Aethra refused to tell Theseus who his father was
  F Aethra refused to speak to Theseus' father [3]

(h) *ad regiam ... vis* (lines 8-9):
  (i) what **two** orders did Aethra give to Theseus? [4]
  (ii) how would this help Theseus? [2]

Total mark for Question 1: [25]

2 Theseus begins his journey, and soon comes upon the first hazard.

Theseus, quamquam Aethra eum in nave Athenas ire iusserat, mare transire nolebat. cibum igitur et gladium portans, matrem reliquit, timore perculsam. latrones, de quibus mater eum monuerat, non timebat. iuvenis enim fortissimus erat.

  prima pars itineris per silvam iacebat. ubi mediae silvae appropinquabat, clamorem audivit. mox hominem ingentem conspexit, qui summam arborem ad terram trahebat. ille, simulac Theseum vidit, clamavit: 'ego sum Sinis. me adiuva.'

  'quid facere vis?' rogavit Theseus.

  'hanc arborem ad terram ligare volo,' Sinis respondit.

  Theseus, quamquam nesciebat cur Sinis hoc facere vellet, eum libenter adiuvit. mox summam arborem ligaverunt. cum Theseus discedere coepisset, homo clamavit: 'mane! alteram arborem ligare cupio.'

Names

Sinis, -is m.   Sinis

Words

timor, -oris m.   fear
percello,-ere, -culi, -culsus   I dismay, strike
latro, -onis m.   robber, bandit
arbor, -oris f.   tree
ligo, -are, -avi   I tie

3 Theseus deals with the first bandit.

1 Theseus hominem iterum adiuvit. mox caput alterius arboris ad
2 terram ligabatur. subito tamen Sinis, simulatque hoc confecerunt,
3 Theseum oppugnavit. quamquam Sinis ferociter pugnavit, Theseus, qui
4 fortior erat, eum ad terram tandem iecit. ubi Theseus intellexit quid Sinis
5 facere vellet, tam iratus erat, ut facere constitueret id quod Sinis facere
6 voluerat: postquam bracchia Sinis ad duas arbores ligavit, funes, qui
7 arbores ad terram tenebant, gladio scidit. homo in duas partes
8 divellebatur.
9   Theseus, gaudens quod latronem crudelissimum superaverat, e silva
10 exiit.

Words

arbor, -oris f.	tree
ligo, -are, -avi	I tie
bracchium, -i n.	arm
funis, -is m.	rope
scindo, -ere, scidi	I cut
divello, -ere	I tear apart
latro, -onis m.	robber, bandit

(a) Which is the correct translation of *Theseus hominem iterum adiuvit* (line 1)?

 A Theseus heard the man again
 B Theseus helped the man again
 C Theseus heard about the man's journey
 D Theseus helped the man on his journey [1]

(b) *mox ... ligabatur* (lines 1-2): what did the two men do? [3]

(c) *subito ... oppugnavit* (lines 2-3):
 (i) what did Sinis do? [2]
 (ii) when did he do this? [2]

(d) *quamquam ... iecit* (lines 3-4): which **three** of the following statements are true? Write down the letters for the ones that are correct.

 A Sinis fought ferociously
 B Theseus attacked Sinis ferociously
 C Sinis was stronger than Theseus
 D Theseus was stronger than Sinis
 E Theseus threw Sinis to the ground
 F Sinis lay down on the ground [3]

(e) *ubi ... voluerat* (lines 4-6):
 (i) what did Theseus understand? [3]
 (ii) write down and translate the Latin adjective that describes how Theseus felt. [2]
 (iii) what did Theseus decide to do as a result of feeling like this? [3]

(f) *postquam ... scidit* (lines 6-7):
 (i) what did Theseus do first? [4]
 (ii) what did he do next? [2]
 (iii) what were the ropes doing before Theseus did these two actions? [2]
 (iv) write down an English word that comes from *terra*. [1]

(g) *homo ... divellebatur* (lines 7-8): what happened to Sinis? [2]

(h) *Theseus ... exiit* (lines 9-10):
   (i) write down and translate the Latin word that describes how Theseus felt. [2]
   (ii) what caused him to feel this way? [3]

Total mark for Question 3: [35]

5   *The story of Theseus (3)*

1   *Theseus has difficulty crossing a river.*

1   Theseus e manibus Sinis effugerat. post paucas horas ad flumen venit.
2   hoc flumen <u>altum</u> erat, quod diu <u>pluerat</u>. Theseus flumen transire non
3   poterat. ibi stabat, cogitans quid facere deberet. subito iuvenis ei
4   appropinquavit.
5   'si flumen transire vis,' inquit iuvenis, 'mecum veni. locum cognovi,
6   ubi flumen est <u>angustum</u>. ibi trans flumen <u>salire</u> possumus.'
7   Theseus iam laetior erat, quod ei non <u>necesse</u> erat prope flumen
8   manere. cum ad partem fluminis <u>angustam</u> pervenissent, iuvenis
9   primum <u>saluit</u>, sed in medium flumen <u>cecidit</u>.

Names

Theseus, -i m.	Theseus	*Sinis, -is* m.	Sinis

Words

altus, -a, -um	deep	*salio, -ire, -ui*	I jump
pluit, -ere, -it	it is raining	*necesse*	necessary
angustus, -a, -um	narrow	*cado, -ere, cecidi*	I fall

(a) Which is the correct translation of *Theseus e manibus Sinis effugerat* (line 1)?
     A Theseus escaped from the hands of Sinis
     B Theseus had escaped from the hands of Sinis
     C Theseus was escaping from the hands of Sinis
     D Theseus escapes from the hands of Sinis [1]

(b) *post ... venit* (lines 1-2): how long did it take Theseus to reach the river? [2]

(c) *hoc ... pluerat* (line 2):
  (i)   write down the Latin word that describes the river.   [1]
  (ii) why was the river like this?   [2]

(d) *Theseus ... poterat* (lines 2-3): what could Theseus not do?   [2]

(e) *ibi ... deberet* (line 3): what did Theseus do? Give full details.   [5]

(f) *subito ... appropinquavit* (lines 3-4): who approached Theseus?   [1]

(g) *si ... possumus* (lines 5-6):
  (i)   what did the speaker tell Theseus to do?   [2]
  (ii) write down an English word that comes from *locum*.   [1]
  (iii) which **three** of the following statements are true? Write down
        the letters for the ones that are correct.
        A the young man knew where the river was narrow
        B the river was narrow in many places
        C only one person could cross the river
        D both Theseus and the young man could cross the river
        E the river could not be crossed although it was narrow
        F the river could be crossed where it was narrow   [3]

(h) *Theseus ... manere* (lines 7-8):
  (i)   write down and translate the Latin word that describes how
        Theseus felt.   [2]
  (ii) why did he feel this way?   [2]

(i) *cum ...cecidit* (lines 8-9): who jumped first?   [1]

Total mark for Question 1: [25]

2   *Theseus survives his second ordeal.*

'me adiuva!' iuvenis clamavit. 'natare non possum.'
    Theseus, qui natare poterat, statim in flumen desiluit. mox iuvenem
tenebat; deinde eum ad ripam traxit. iuvenis tam gratus erat, ut Theseo
narrare constitueret, qualis vir dominus esset.
    'meus dominus,' inquit, 'est Procrustes. Procrustes est homo
crudelissimus. me ad flumen misit, ut viatorem quaererem et ad villam
nostram invitarem. hospites tamen semper necat. tibi necesse est eum
interficere.'

117

postquam ad villam Procrustis advenerunt, Procrustes Theseo cenam libenter paravit; deinde eum ad cubiculum duxit. ibi Theseo persuasit, ut in cubili iaceret.

'tu longior es quam cubile,' Procrustes dixit. 'necesse est mihi pedes tuos abscidere.'

Names

Procrustes, -is m.   Procrustes

Words

nato, -are	I swim	hospes, -itis m.	guest
desilio, -ire, -ui	I jump down	necesse	necessary
ripa, -ae f.	river bank	cubiculum, -i n.	bedroom
gratus, -a, -um	grateful	cubile, -is n.	bed
viator, -oris m.	traveller	abscido, -ere	I cut off
invito, -are	I invite		

[40]

3   *Theseus arrives safely in Athens, after dealing with Procrustes.*

1 Procrustes, quod homo crudelissimus erat, Theseum necare
2 volebat. bipennem igitur, quam sub cubili celaverat, statim sustulit ut
3 Theseum oppugnaret. sed Theseus, qui multo valentior erat quam
4 Procrustes, postquam bipennem e manibus eius rapuit, eum facile
5 superavit. mox Procrustes ipse in cubili iacebat, sine pedibus suis. ille
6 servus, qui Theseum ad villam duxerat, erat laetissimus, quod Theseus
7 dominum necaverat et mors domini eum liberaverat.
8   postridie Theseus iuvenem gaudentem ac dominum mortuum
9 sepelientem reliquit, ut iter ad urbem Athenas faceret. duos post dies ad
10 urbem advenit.

Name

Athenae, -arum f.pl.   Athens

Words

bipennis, -is f.	axe	valens, -ntis	strong
cubile, -is n.	bed	mortuus, -a, -um	dead
tollo, -ere, sustuli	I pick up	sepelio, -ire	I bury

118

(a) Write down and translate the Latin word in line 1 that describes the man Procrustes. [3]

(b) *Theseum necare volebat* (lines 1-2): what did Procrustes want to do? [2]

(c) *bipennem ... oppugnaret* (lines 2-3): which **three** of the following statements are true? Write down the letters for the ones that are correct.
- A   an axe stood by the bed
- B   Procrustes picked up an axe
- C   Procrustes had hidden the axe
- D   Procrustes had hidden under the bed
- E   Theseus wanted to attack Procrustes
- F   Procrustes wanted to attack Theseus [3]

(d) *sed Theseus ... superavit* (lines 3-5):
- (i)   how is Theseus described here? [3]
- (ii)   how did Theseus get the better of Procrustes? [2]
- (iii)   was the struggle long or short? Give a reason for your answer. [1]

(e) *mox ... suis* (line 5): what happened to Procrustes? Give full details. [3]

(f) *ille servus ... liberaverat* (lines 5-7):
- (i)   *qui ... duxerat*: what are we told here about Procrustes' slave? [3]
- (ii)   write down and translate the Latin word that tells us how the slave felt. [3]
- (iii)   why did he feel this way? Give **two** reasons. [5]

(g) *postridie ... faceret* (lines 8-9):
- (i)   what two things was the young man doing when Theseus left? [3]
- (ii)   which is the correct translation of *ut iter ad Athenas faceret*?
  - A   and he travelled to Athens
  - B   in order to travel to Athens
  - C   to go to Athens again
  - D   so that he went to Athens [1]

(h) *duos ... advenit* (lines 9-10):
- (i)   how long did the journey take? [2]
- (ii)   write down an English word that comes from *urbem*. [1]

Total mark for Question 3: [35]

6 The story of Theseus (4)

1 Theseus reaches the palace in Athens.

1 Theseus erat iuvenis fortis, qui duos <u>latrones</u> iam superaverat.
2 Theseus ad urbem Athenas iter faciebat, quod cognoscere volebat, quis
3 pater esset. simulatque ad urbem advenit, <u>regiam</u> quaesivit. <u>regia</u> in
4 media urbe erat. Theseus, cum ad <u>regiam</u> advenisset, servum, qui
5 ianuam aperuit, iussit se ad regem ducere. servus eum prope ianuam
6 reliquit, ut regem peteret. sed ubi servus rediit, <u>regina</u>, non rex, cum eo
7 venit. <u>regina</u>, cuius nomen erat Medea, Theseum <u>intente</u> spectavit;
8 gladium quem gerebat quoque conspexit.

Names

Theseus, -i m.	Theseus	*Athenae, -arum* f.pl.	Athens
Medea, -ae f.	Medea		

Words

latro, -onis m.	robber, bandit
regia, -ae f.	royal palace
regina, -ae f.	queen
intente	closely

(a) *Theseus ... fortis* (line 1): how is Theseus described here? [2]

(b) *qui ... superaverat* (line 1): what had Theseus done? [2]

(c) *Theseus ... esset* (lines 2-3): why was Theseus travelling to Athens? [4]

(d) *simulatque ... erat* (lines 3-4):
   (i) what did Theseus do as soon as he reached Athens? [2]
   (ii) to which part of the city did he go? [1]
   (iii) write down an English word that comes from *mediam*. [1]

(e) *Theseus ... ducere* (lines 4-5): which **two** of the following statements are true? Write down the letters for the ones that are correct.
   A   a slave opened the door
   B   Theseus opened the door
   C   the slave ordered Theseus to go inside
   D   Theseus ordered the slave to take him to the king [2]

(f) *servus ... peteret* (lines 5-6):
    (i)   where did the slave leave Theseus? [2]
    (ii) why did the slave leave? [2]

(g) *sed ... venit* (lines 6-7): in what way did Theseus fail to achieve his wish? [2]

(h) *regina ... conspexit* (lines 7-8):
    (i)   which is the correct translation of *cuius nomen erat Medea*?
        A her name was Medea
        B which was the name of Medea
        C which was named Medea
        D whose name was Medea [1]
    (ii) what **two** things did the queen do? [4]

Total mark for Question 1: [25]

2   *Medea invites Theseus into the palace.*

Medea, postquam Theseum spectavit, tandem ei dixit:
   'rex Aegeus abest. si eum videre vis, ad cenam veni. nunc abi.'
Theseus igitur per urbem ambulavit, ut templa pulchra spectaret. tribus post horis ad <u>regiam</u> rediit, gladium gerens. <u>regina</u> ipsa ianuam aperuit et eum in <u>regiam</u> accepit.
Medea tamen consilium dirum ceperat, quod, simulac gladium conspexit, cognoverat quis Theseus esset. maritus enim eius illum gladium reliquerat, ubi amicum <u>visitabat</u>.
   'visne vinum <u>bibere</u>?' rogavit <u>regina</u>. <u>poculum</u> Theseo statim tradidit. sed <u>antequam</u> Theseus vinum <u>bibere</u> poterat, rex subito intravit. is quoque, simulac gladium vidit, intellexit quis esset Theseus. deinde rex <u>poculum</u>, quod Theseus tenebat, conspexit.

Names

Aegeus, -i m.   Aegeus

Words

regia, -ae f.	royal palace	*bibo, -ere*	I drink
regina, -ae f.	queen	*poculum, -i* n.	wine-cup
visito, -are	I visit	*antequam*	before

[40]

3   *Theseus finally meets his father.*

1   Aegeus, ubi <u>poculum</u> conspexit, perterritus erat. illud <u>poculum</u> enim
2   <u>agnovit</u>, quod uxor saepe <u>venenum</u> in eo posuerat. statim intellexit quid
3   uxor faceret et cur iuvenem necare vellet. uxor enim, quae quoque
4   gladium <u>agnoverat</u>, <u>invida</u> erat, quod alia femina marito filium
5   praebuerat.
6   rex, clamans 'noli <u>bibere</u>', ad Theseum cucurrit et <u>poculum</u> ad terram
7   <u>deiecit</u>. terra, vino <u>tacta</u>, <u>ferbuit</u>. Theseus ibi stabat, <u>attonitus</u>.
8   rex ei dixit, 'tu es filius meus. quam laetus sum te videre! sed tu,
9   Medea, eum occidere volebas. abi! nolo te iterum videre!'
10   Theseus gaudebat, quod iam cognoverat quis esset pater.

Words

poculum, -i n.	wine-cup
agnosco, -ere, agnovi	I recognise
venenum, -i n.	poison
invidus, -a, -um	jealous
bibo, -ere	I drink
deicio, -ere, deieci	I knock down
tango, -ere, tetigi, tactus	I touch
ferveo, -ere, ferbui	I steam, boil
attonitus, -a, -um	astonished

(a) *Aegeus ... erat* (line 1):
   (i)   write down and translate the Latin word that tells us how Aegeus
         felt.   [2]
   (ii) when did he feel like this?   [1]

(b) *illud ... posuerat* (lines 1-2): how was Aegeus able to recognise the
    cup?   [4]

(c) *statim ... vellet* (lines 2-3): what **two** things did Aegeus immediately
    realise?   [6]

(d) *uxor enim ... praebuerat* (lines 3-5): which **three** of the following statements are true? Write down the letters for the ones that are correct.

    A Medea had recognised the sword
    B Aegeus recognised his son
    C Aegeus was jealous
    D Medea was jealous
    E another woman had provided a son for Aegeus
    F another woman had married her son   [3]

(e) *rex ... deiecit* (lines 6-7):
    (i)   which is the correct translation of *noli bibere*?
        A he did not drink
        B he did not want to drink
        C you do not want to drink
        D don't drink   [1]
    (ii) what **two** things did the king do?   [4]

(f) *terra, vino tacta, ferbuit* (line 7): explain in your own words what happened here.   [3]

(g) *Theseus ibi stabat, attonitus* (line 7): write down the Latin word that describes Theseus.   [1]

(h) *rex ... te videre* (line 8):
    (i)   what revelation did the king make?   [2]
    (ii) what did he say made him *laetus*?   [1]

(i) *sed ... iterum videre* (lines 8-9):
    (i)   what did the king think Medea wanted to do?   [1]
    (ii) what did he order her to do?   [1]
    (iii) how did he make it clear that their relationship was over?   [3]

(j) *Theseus ... pater* (line 10): why was Theseus pleased?   [2]

Total mark for Question 3: [35]

7   Romulus and Remus (1)

1   *There is a dispute over who should be king of Alba Longa.*

1   Numitor et Amulius erant filii regis Albae Longae. post mortem patris
2   eorum, Numitor, quod <u>senior</u> erat, rex esse debebat. Amulius tamen,
3   qui vir crudelis erat, fratrem ex urbe <u>expulit</u> ut rex ipse esset. deinde
4   Amulius, postquam filios Numitoris necavit, filiam eius, Rheam Silviam
5   nomine, coegit Virginem Vestalem esse. poena erat mors Virgini
6   Vestali, quae cum viro dormiebat.
7   quamquam Amulius tantum fecit, ut <u>aemulos</u> <u>removeret</u>, Rhea Silvia
8   duos filios <u>peperit</u>. hi filii erant Romulus et Remus.

Names

Numitor, -oris m.	Numitor
Amulius, -i m.	Amulius
Alba Longa, Albae Longae f.	Alba Longa (a city near Rome)
Rhea Silvia, Rheae Silviae f.	Rhea Silvia
Virgo Vestalis, Virginis Vestalis f.	Vestal Virgin (priestess of the goddess Vesta)
Romulus, -i m.	Romulus
Remus, -i m.	Remus

Words

senior, -ius	elder
expello, -ere, -puli	I drive out
aemulus, -i m.	rival
removeo, -ere	I remove
pario, -ere, peperi	I give birth to

(a) *Numitor ... Albae Longae* (line 1): how were Numitor and Amulius
  related?   [1]

(b) *post ... debebat* (lines 1-2):
  (i)   what happened to the old king?   [1]
  (ii) what ought to have happened next?   [2]
  (iii) why was this?   [1]
  (iv) write down an English word that comes from *mortem*.   [1]

(c) *Amulius ... esset* (lines 2-3): which **three** of the following statements are true? Write down the letters for the ones that are correct.

    A Amulius was a cruel man
    B Numitor was a cruel man
    C Amulius was driven out by his brother
    D Numitor was driven out by his brother
    E Amulius acted in order to become king
    F Numitor acted in order to become king   [3]

(d) *deinde ... esse* (lines 3-5):
    (i)   what happened to Numitor's sons?   [2]
    (ii) who was Rhea Silvia?   [1]
    (iii) what happened to her?   [3]

(e) *poena ... dormiebat* (lines 5-6):
    (i)   what punishment for a Vestal Virgin is mentioned here?   [1]
    (ii) why would this punishment be given?   [2]

(f) *quamquam ... peperit* (lines 7-8):
    (i)   which is the correct translation of *quamquam Amulius tantum fecit*?
        A although Amulius made so many things
        B although Amulius made this
        C although Amulius did this
        D although Amulius did so much   [1]
    (ii) why did he do this?   [1]
    (iii) how did Rhea Silvia hinder Amulius' plan?   [3]
    (iv) how do you think this would have made Amulius feel?   [1]
    (v) explain your answer to (iv).   [1]

Total mark for Question 1: [25]

2   *Amulius tries to kill Romulus and Remus, but fails.*

cum Amulius Rheam Silviam rogavisset, quis esset pater duorum filiorum, illa respondit, 'Mars.' rex iratus, postquam eam in <u>carcerem</u> iecit, pueros militibus tradidit, ut eos in flumine necarent. milites tamen, quod hoc facere nolebant, pueros in <u>canistro</u> posuerunt; hoc magna cum cura in flumine posuerunt, deos orantes ut pueros servarent. post tres horas flumen <u>canistrum</u> ad <u>ripam</u> tulit. ibi <u>lupa</u>, quae de montibus ad flumen venerat, ut aquam <u>biberet</u>, pueros lacrimantes audivit. <u>lupa</u> pueris, quos e <u>canistro</u> in silvam portaverat, <u>lac</u> praebuit. ita Romulus

Remusque servabantur. tandem <u>pastor</u> eos inventos ad uxorem portavit; quae eos multos annos <u>educabat</u>.

Names

Mars, -tis m.	Mars (God of War)

Words

carcer, -eris m.	prison
canistrum, -i n.	basket
ripa, -ae f.	bank (of a river)
lupa, -ae f.	she-wolf
bibo, -ere	I drink
lac, -tis n.	milk
pastor, -oris m.	shepherd
educo, -are	I bring up

[40]

3 Read the passage below and answer the questions that follow.

Romulus and Remus beat robbers at their own game.

1 Romulus et Remus, ubi iuvenes erant, saepe <u>latrones</u>
2 oppugnabant, ut <u>praedam</u> eorum raperent. omnem <u>praedam</u> inter
3 <u>pastores</u> <u>dividebant</u>. tot alii iuvenes, cum haec cognovissent, convenire
4 coeperunt, ut mox turba iuvenum esset, qui etiam plures <u>latrones</u>
5 oppugnabant. tandem <u>latrones</u> tam irati erant, ut <u>insidias</u> contra iuvenes
6 facerent. quamquam Romulus eis fortiter restitit, <u>latrones</u> Remum
7 captum ad Amulium traxerunt.
8   'hic iuvenis,' inquiunt <u>latrones</u>, 'manum iuvenum contra <u>agros</u>
9 Numitoris ducebat.'
10   Amulius, qui nec <u>latronibus</u> nec Remo credidit, Numitori iuvenem
11 tradidit ut poenas daret.

Words

latro, -onis m.	robber, bandit
praeda, -ae f.	booty, loot
pastor, -oris m.	shepherd
divido, -ere	I divide
insidiae, -arum f.pl.	ambush
ager, agri m.	land

(a) *Romulus ... raperent* (lines 1-2):
    (i) what did Romulus and Remus often do when they grew up? [2]
    (ii) why did they do this? [2]

(b) *omnem ... dividebant* (lines 2-3): how did Romulus and Remus help the shepherds? [2]

(c) *tot ... oppugnabant* (lines 3-5): which **four** of the following statements are true? Write down the letters for the ones that are correct.
    A lots of young men joined Romulus and Remus
    B all the others joined the young men
    C Romulus and Remus found this out
    D the young men learned what Romulus and Remus were doing
    E soon the young men joined a crowd
    F soon a crowd of young men had developed
    G even more young men attacked the bandits
    H the young men attacked even more bandits [4]

(d) *tandem ... facerent* (lines 5-6):
    (i) write down and translate the Latin word that describes how the bandits felt. [2]
    (ii) why do you think they felt this way? [1]
    (iii) what did they do as a result of feeling like this? [3]

(e) *quamquam ... traxerunt* (lines 6-7):
    (i) what did Romulus do? [2]
    (ii) what happened to Remus? [3]

(f) *hic ... ducebat* (lines 8-9):
    (i) what did the bandits accuse Remus of doing? [4]
    (ii) was their accusation truthful? Explain your answer. [2]

(g) *Amulius ... daret* (lines 10-11):
    (i) write down and translate the Latin word that refers to Remus without naming him. [2]
    (ii) what action did Amulius take? [2]
    (iii) what caused him to do this? [3]
    (iv) what did he expect to happen to Remus? [1]

Total mark for Question 3: [35]

8 *Romulus and Remus (2)*

1 *Numitor realises who Remus is.*

1 Romulus et Remus erant fratres. Remus, a <u>latronibus</u> captus, ad
2 Numitorem ducebatur. Numitor, ubi verba <u>latronum</u> audivit, cogitabat
3 num Remus poenas dare deberet. sed <u>latronibus</u> non credebat. simulac
4 Remum conspexit et de fratre eius cognovit, <u>attonitus</u> erat.
5   'quis est pater tuus?' Numitor rogavit, iam plenus spei.
6   'nescio,' respondit Remus. '<u>lupa</u> nos <u>infantes</u> e flumine servavit.
7 deinde <u>pastor</u> et uxor eius nos <u>educabant</u>.
8   duo <u>nepotes</u>, quos frater Amulius in flumine necare voluerat, statim
9 in animum Numitoris venerunt; iam erat laetissimus.

Names

Romulus, -i m.	Romulus	*Remus, -i* m.	Remus
Numitor, -oris m.	Numitor	*Amulius, -i* m.	Amulius

Words

latro, -onis m.	robber, bandit	*pastor, -oris* m.	shepherd
attonitus, -a, -um	astonished	*educo, -are*	I bring up
lupa, -ae f.	she-wolf	*nepos, -otis* m.	grandson
infans, -ntis m.	baby		

(a) *Romulus ... fratres* (line 1): what are we told about Romulus and
    Remus?   [1]

(b) *Remus ... ducebatur* (lines 1-2):
    (i)   what had previously happened to Remus?   [2]
    (ii) what was happening to him now?   [2]

(c) *Numitor ... deberet* (lines 2-3):
    (i)   which is the correct translation of *ubi verba latronum audivit*?
         A where the words of the bandits were heard
         B when the words of the bandits were heard
         C where he heard the words of the bandits
         D when he heard the words of the bandits   [1]
    (ii) what did Numitor consider?   [2]

(d) *sed ... credebat* (line 3): what was Numitor's attitude towards the
    bandits?   [1]

(e) *simulac ... erat* (lines 3-4): which **three** of the following statements are true? Write down the letters for the ones that are correct.
    A Numitor caught sight of Remus
    B Remus caught sight of Numitor
    C Remus found out about Numitor's brother
    D Numitor found out about Remus' brother
    E Numitor was astonished
    F Remus was astonished   [3]

(f) *quis ... spei* (line 5):
    (i)   what question did Numitor ask?   [2]
    (ii) write down and translate the **two** Latin words that describe
         Numitor.   [3]

(g) *'nescio,' respondit Remus* (line 6): what was Remus' reply?   [1]

(h) *lupa ... educabant* (lines 6-7): describe the boys' early childhood and upbringing.   [4]

(i) *duo ... laetissimus* (lines 8-9):
    (i)   what image came into Numitor's mind?   [1]
    (ii) what should have happened to the boys?   [1]
    (iii) why do you think Numitor felt *laetissimus*?   [1]

Total mark for Question 1: [25]

2   *Romulus and Remus avenge Numitor and make him king.*

Remus, cum cognovisset quid Amulius fecisset, iratissimus erat. statim Remus cum fratre ceterisque iuvenibus Amulium et amicos tam ferociter oppugnavit, ut brevissimo tempore regem occiderent. deinde Numitor civibus convocatis narravit omnia quae acciderat. ubi Romulus Remusque per turbam ambulantes Numitorem regem salutaverunt, cives gaudentes <u>plauserunt</u>.
    cum Numitor esset rex Albae Longae, Romulus et Remus sibi novam urbem aedificare volebant, prope flumen in quo <u>lupa</u> eos invenerat. sed quod fratres erant <u>gemini</u>, difficile erat constituere <u>uter</u> dux esse deberet. deos igitur oraverunt ut sibi signum darent. quamquam Remus sex <u>vultures</u> a deis missos vidit, Romulus <u>duodecim</u> conspexit. Romulus igitur a civibus rex salutabatur.

Names

Alba Longa, Albae Longae f.   Alba Longa (a city near Rome)

Words

plaudo, -ere, -si	I clap, applaud
lupa, -ae f.	she-wolf
gemini, -orum m. pl.	twins
uter, -ra, -rum	which one
vultur, -uris m.	vulture
duodecim	twelve

Total mark for Question 2: [40]

3   *Romulus and Remus quarrel, with fatal results.*

1   Remus non erat laetus, quod frater, non ipse, iam dux erat inter cives
2   novae urbis. hoc accipere nolebat. ubi muros urbis conspexit, quos
3   Romulus et amici eius aedificabant, eos <u>sprevit</u>.
4   'ecce!' clamavit Remus, 'hi muri sunt minimi: ego facile possum eos
5   <u>transilire</u>.'
6   Romulus tam iratus erat, cum fratrem muros <u>transilientem</u> vidisset, ut
7   eum statim necaret. ita Romulus solus imperium habebat. cives urbi
8   novae nomen 'Romam' dederunt, quod fideles Romulo erant. paucis
9   annis haec urbs <u>potentior</u> erat quam omnes aliae.

Words

sperno, -ere, sprevi	I mock, laugh at
ecce!	look!
transilio, -ire	I jump over
potens, -ntis	powerful

(a) *Remus ... urbis* (lines 1-2): why was Remus unhappy?   [5]

(b) Which is the correct translation of *hoc accipere nolebat* (line 2)?
        A   he didn't want to receive this
        B   he refused to accept this
        C   this was accepted knowledge
        D   he received this knowledge   [1]

(c) *ubi ... sprevit* (lines 2-3): which **three** of the following statements are
true? Write down the letters for the ones that are correct.

      A   Remus caught sight of the city walls
      B   Romulus caught sight of the city walls
      C   Romulus was building the walls for his friends
      D   Romulus and his friends were building the walls
      E   Remus mocked the walls
      F   Romulus mocked the walls   [3]

(d) *ecce ... transilire* (lines 4-5):
    (i)   write down and translate the Latin word that describes the
         walls.   [3]
    (ii) write down an English word that comes from *facile*.   [1]
    (iii) what did Remus say he could easily do?   [1]

(e) *Romulus ... necaret* (lines 6-7):
    (i)   how did Romulus feel?   [1]
    (ii) why did he feel this way?   [3]
    (iii) what did he do as a result?   [2]

(f) *ita ... habebat* (line 7): how did Romulus' situation change?   [3]

(g) *cives ... erant* (lines 7-8):
    (i)   what did the citizens do?   [3]
    (ii) why did they do this?   [3]

(h) *paucis ... aliae* (lines 8-9):
    (i)   how long did it take for things to change?   [2]
    (ii) how did Rome change in that time?   [4]

Total mark for Question 3: [35]

9 *How the new city of Rome gained citizens*

1 *Romulus' new city, called Rome, lacks citizens, and so he attracts*
  young men from the surrounding lands.

1 Romulus erat dux novae urbis. Romulus, quamquam paucos
2 amicos habebat, qui eum adiuverant ut Amulium vinceret, plures cives
3 habere cupiebat. in urbe igitur <u>asylum</u> aperuit. multi homines ab urbibus
4 <u>finitimis</u> ad <u>asylum</u> mox fugiebant. horum hominum multi erant servi, qui
5 a dominis effugerant; alii <u>scelesti</u> erant, qui pecuniam abstulerant <u>aut</u>
6 homines occiderant. Romulus omnes libenter accipiebat. sed erant
7 nullae feminae. brevi tempore Romulus cogitare coepit, quo modo
8 feminis persuadere posset, ut ad urbem venirent.

Names

Romulus, -i m.	Romulus
Amulius, -i m.	Amulius

Words

asylum, -i n.	refuge, safe area
finitimus, -a, -um	neighbouring
scelestus, -a, -um	wicked
aut	or

(a) How is Romulus described in the first sentence? [3]

(b) *Romulus, quamquam ... cupiebat* (lines 1-3): which **three** of the
  following statements are true? Write down the letters for the ones that
  are correct.
  A   Romulus had a few friends
  B   Romulus had more than a few friends
  C   the friends had helped Romulus to defeat Amulius
  D   Romulus had helped his friends to defeat Amulius
  E   more citizens wanted to live there
  F   Romulus wanted to have more citizens [3]

(c) *in urbe ... aperuit* (line 3): what did Romulus do? [2]

(d) *multi ... fugiebant* (lines 3-4): explain how the new city gained more
  citizens. [4]

(e) *horum ... occiderant* (lines 4-6): give full details of the two groups of
  people who came to the city. [6]

(f) Which is the correct translation of *Romulus omnes libenter accipiebat* (line 6)?

    A Romulus had accepted them all gladly

    B they all received Romulus gladly

    C Romulus accepted them all gladly

    D Romulus accepted all the freedmen   [1]

(g) *sed ... feminae* (lines 6-7): what problem was there?   [2]

(h) *brevi ... venirent* (lines 7-8): what did Romulus start to consider?   [4]

Total mark for Question 1: [25]

2   *Romulus now solves the problem of the shortage of women.*

iam erant multi viri in urbe Roma, sed nullae feminae. Romulus igitur nuntios ad omnes urbes <u>finitimas</u> misit, ut cives Romam ad magnum <u>spectaculum</u> invitarent. plurimae <u>familiae</u> a multis urbibus Romam iter fecerunt, non solum ut <u>spectaculum</u> sed etiam ut novam urbem viderent. Romani eos in domos suas laete acceperunt. cum novum forum et omnia templa conspexissent, <u>attoniti</u> erant, quod urbs tam celeriter <u>creverat</u>. ubi omnes parati erant <u>spectaculum</u> spectare, Romulus signum dedit. subito iuvenes Romani ad <u>familias</u> cucurrerunt. omnes <u>virgines</u>, quae cum <u>parentibus</u> Romam venerant, raptas ad domos suas portaverunt. <u>parentes</u> earum, qui nulla <u>arma</u> secum habebant, discesserunt tristissimi. iuvenes Romani nunc uxores habebant.

Words

finitimus, -a, -um	neighbouring	*cresco, -ere, crevi*	I grow
spectaculum, -i n.	show, games	*virgo, -inis* f.	maiden, young
invito, -are	I invite		woman
familia, -ae f.	family	*parens, -ntis* m.	parent
attonitus, -a, -um	astonished	*arma, -orum* n.pl.	arms, weapons

Total mark for Question 2: [40]

3   *Peace is finally achieved.*

1   <u>parentes</u>, quorum filias Romani abstulerant, tam irati erant ut
2   ducibus urbium suarum persuaderent, ut Romam oppugnarent. Romani
3   tamen eos facile vicerunt. novae uxores Romanorum, quamquam
4   iuvenes eas tam crudeliter rapuerant, iam laetiores erant, quod mariti
5   eis amorem et dona et pulchras domos dederant. feminae igitur, cum
6   <u>parentes</u> iterum cum maiore <u>exercitu</u> advenissent, in medium <u>proelium</u>
7   cucurrerunt, patres maritosque orantes ut pacem facerent.
8   'nos,' inquiunt, 'sumus <u>causa</u> belli. in nos iram gladiosque vertite.
9   melius est nobis perire quam sine maritis, sine patribus vivere.'
10   postquam haec verba audiverunt, duces pacem fecerunt.

Words

parens, -ntis m.	parent	*proelium, -i* n.	battle
exercitus, -us m.	army	*causa, -ae* f.	cause

(a) *parentes ... oppugnarent* (lines 1-2):
   (i)   what had happened to the daughters? [2]
   (ii) how did that make their parents feel? [1]
   (iii) what did the parents do as a result? [5]

(b) *Romani ... vicerunt* (lines 2-3): what happened in this first battle? [2]

(c) *novae ... dederant* (lines 3-5):
   (i)   write down and translate the Latin adjective that tells us how the new wives of the Romans felt. [3]
   (ii) what was surprising about the fact that they felt this way? [2]
   (iii) why did they feel this way? [5]

(d) *feminae ... facerent* (lines 5-7):
   (i)   which **four** of the following statements are true? Write down the letters for the ones that are correct.
       A the parents of the women were travelling
       B the parents of the women arrived again
       C they had a larger army than before
       D they had a better army than before
       E the parents ran into the middle of the battle
       F the women ran into the middle of the battle
       G the fathers were begging the husbands
       H the women were begging fathers and husbands [4]
   (ii) write down an English word that comes from *maritos*. [1]

(e) Which is the correct translation of *nos sumus causa belli* (line 8)?
    A we are the cause of the war
    B our war is a just cause
    C the war has caused us to be here
    D our beauty is the cause   [1]

(f) *in nos ... vertite* (line 8):
    (i)   who is / are speaking these words?   [1]
    (ii) what **two** groups are being addressed?   [2]
    (iii) what are these two groups being told to do? [2]

(g) *melius ... vivere* (line 9): what is the argument here?   [3]

(h) *postquam ... fecerunt* (line 10): what was the final outcome?   [1]

Total mark for Question 3: [35]

10 *The story of Lars Porsenna*

1   *The Etruscans, thrown out of Rome, seek the help of Porsenna.*

1   Lars Porsenna erat rex Clusii. haec urbs, quam Etrusci multis annis
2   antea aedificaverant, iam magnum imperium habebat. Porsenna ipse
3   erat Etruscus. ubi Romani, post longum bellum, regem suum,
4   Tarquinium, <u>expulerunt</u>, ille, quod erat Etruscus, ad Porsennam
5   festinavit, ut auxilium eius peteret.
6   'ego,' inquit, 'sum Etruscus; tu quoque es Etruscus. nos <u>una</u>
7   pugnare debemus.'
8   Porsenna, qui imperium <u>crescens</u> Romae timebat, libenter
9   <u>consensit</u>. magnum <u>exercitum</u> igitur in <u>agros</u> Romanorum duxit. tanta
10 erat <u>fama</u> Porsennae, ut Romani timerent.

Names

Lars Porsenna, Lartis Porsennae m.	Lars Porsenna
Clusium, -i n.	Clusium (a city near Rome)
Etrusci, -orum m.pl.	the Etruscans (a race of people who lived in central Italy)
Etruscus, -a, -um	Etruscan
Tarquinius, -i m.	Tarquinius (the last king of Rome)

Words

expello, -ere, -puli	I drive out
una	together

cresco, -ere	I grow
consentio, -ire, -sensi	I agree
exercitus, -us m.	army
agri, -orum m.pl.	territory
fama, -ae f.	reputation

(a) *Lars ...Clusii* (line 1): who was Lars Porsenna? [1]

(b) *haec ... habebat* (lines 1-2):
   (i)   what are we told about the previous history of Clusium? [3]
   (ii) what was it like now? [2]

(c) *ubi ... peteret* (lines 3-5): which **four** of the following statements are true? Write down the letters for the ones that are correct.
   A   the Romans fought a long war
   B   there was a long war after these events
   C   the Romans drove out their king
   D   the Roman king drove out Tarquinius
   E   Tarquinius was a king of Clusium
   F   Tarquinius went to Porsenna because Porsenna was Etruscan
   G   Porsenna wanted Tarquinius' help
   H   Tarquinius wanted Porsenna's help [4]

(d) *ego ... debemus* (lines 6-7):
   (i)   who speaks these words? [1]
   (ii) what does the speaker think they should do? [1]
   (iii) what reason does he give for this? [1]

(e) *Porsenna ... consensit* (lines 8-9):
   (i)   why was Porsenna ready to do as he was asked? [3]
   (ii) write down and translate the Latin word that tells us how keen Porsenna was to do as he was asked. [2]

(f) *magnum ... duxit* (line 9): what did Porsenna do? [3]

(g) *tanta ... timerent* (lines 9-10):
   (i)   what effect did Porsenna have when he arrived? [2]
   (ii) why did he have this effect? [2]

Total mark for Question 1: [25]

136

2   *Porsenna attacks Rome but the only way in is defended by Horatius.*

cum Porsenna Romae appropinquaret, omnes cives Romani ex <u>agris</u> in urbem fugerunt. quamquam Porsenna urbem vehementer oppugnavit, intrare non poterat, quod pars urbis muris, pars flumine <u>muniebatur</u>. sed unus <u>pons</u> erat, qui hostibus viam ad mediam urbem dare poterat. pauci milites Romani hunc <u>pontem</u> <u>custodiebant</u>; simulatque hostes ex <u>agris</u> ad <u>pontem</u> currentes conspexerunt, fugere coeperunt. Horatius tamen, qui forte aderat, eos oravit ut manerent.

   'si vultis,' inquit, 'omnes hostes in media urbe nostra videre, fugite; si tamen <u>libertatem</u> cupitis, mecum manete <u>pontem</u>que delete.'

   Romani, his verbis victi, <u>pontem</u> gladiis manibusque delere coeperunt. interea Horatius in <u>ponte</u> solus stabat, hostes exspectans.

Name

Horatius, -i m.   Horatius

Words

ager, -ri m.	field
munio, -ire	I defend
pons, -tis m.	bridge
custodio, -ire	I guard
libertas, -atis f.	freedom

Total mark for Question 2: [40]

3   *Porsenna is defeated by the bravery first of Horatius, then of Mucius.*

1   Horatius hostibus diu resistebat. ubi tandem <u>pons</u> <u>decidebat</u>, in flumen
2   <u>desiluit</u>. iam Porsenna flumen transire non poterat.
3   deinde Porsenna urbem <u>obsidere</u> coepit. multos post dies iuvenis
4   Romanus, Mucius nomine, Porsennam occidere constituit. regi
5   comitibusque <u>clam</u> appropinquavit sed, cum nesciret quis esset rex,
6   non regem sed <u>scribam</u> eius necavit. Porsenna militibus imperavit ut
7   iuvenem captum necarent.
8   'me necare potes,' clamavit Mucius, 'sed sunt multi alii iuvenes
9   Romani, qui te necare volunt. <u>necesse</u> est tibi semper <u>cavere</u>.'
10   Porsenna tam perterritus erat, ut milites suos ab urbe statim duceret.
11   numquam iterum Romam oppugnavit.

Names

Mucius, -i m.   Mucius

Words

pons, -tis m.	bridge
decido, -ere, -cidi	I fall down
desilio, -ire, -ui	I jump down
obsideo, -ere	I besiege, blockade
clam	furtively
scriba, -ae m.	secretary
necesse	necessary
caveo, -ere	I watch out, am careful

(a) *Horatius ... resistebat* (line 1): write down and translate the Latin word
that tells us how long Horatius resisted.   [2]

(b) Which is the best translation of *ubi tandem pons decidebat* (line 1)?
        A   when however the bridge began to fall down
        B   when the bridge was finally falling down
        C   when the bridge had finally fallen down
        D   however, when the bridge was falling down   [1]

(c) *iam ... poterat* (line 2): what effect did the collapse of the bridge
have?   [4]

(d) *deinde ... coepit* (line 3): what happened next?   [2]

(e) *multos ... constituit* (lines 3-4):
  (i)   which **three** of the following statements are true? Write down the
        letters for the ones that are correct.
          A   many gods stood behind them
          B   many days passed
          C   Mucius was a young Roman
          D   the Romans gave the name Mucius to many young men
          E   Porsenna decided to kill Mucius
          F   Mucius decided to kill Porsenna   [3]
  (ii) write down an English word that comes from *multos*.   [1]

(f) *regi ... necavit* (lines 4-6):
  (i)   which is the correct translation of *regi comitibusque*
        appropinquavit?
          A   the king approached his companions
          B   the king and his companions approached
          C   he approached the king and his companions
          D   the king and his companions were approached   [1]
  (ii) what problem did Mucius have?   [3]
  (iii) what happened as a result of this problem?   [2]

(g) *Porsenna ... necarent* (lines 6-7): what did Porsenna do?   [4]

(h) *me ... volunt* (lines 8-9):
  (i)   what did Mucius tell Porsenna to do?   [1]
  (ii) what threat did Mucius make to Porsenna?   [6]

(i) *Porsenna ... oppugnavit* (lines 10-11):
  (i)   write down the Latin word that describes Porsenna.   [1]
  (ii) what did Porsenna do?   [3]
  (iii) what did he not do again?   [1]

                                   Total mark for Question 3: [35]

Section 6. Tests for WJEC Level 2 Additional and GCSE Higher Tier

Introduction

These tests are all split into two parts, of which the first is for comprehension and the second for translation, giving a ratio of 20:30. The storylines are taken either from history or from mythology. The tests are modelled on those set for the WJEC Level 2 Additional unit, which has determined the ratio of marks, the range of question styles and the glossing of vocabulary. The A402 Higher Tear GCSE unit is almost identical, with a few variations in defined vocabulary and in the ratio of marks, which should be 20:40. The mark schemes for the translations are also based on the WJEC Level 2 format; teachers preparing students for the GCSE may wish to use the type of mark scheme applied by OCR, which is to divide the passage into 10 sections, each worth 4 marks. This is a much cruder system but is quick to apply.

In each exercise, read the first part of the story and answer the questions that follow. Then translate the second part of the story.

1 The conspiracy of Catilina

1 Catilina plots against Rome.

1 Catilina erat senator Romanus, qui consul esse diu voluerat. cum
2 tamen cives Romani Ciceronem, non Catilinam, consulem legissent,
3 Catilina, exercitu hominum pessimorum parato, coniurationem contra
4 senatum facere coepit. Catilina et ceteri duces coniurationis in domum
5 amici convenerunt, ut consilium caperent. duos homines iusserunt
6 postridie prima hora ad domum Ciceronis ire ad eum necandum. Cicero
7 tamen, quod ab uno ex coniuratis rem cognovit, domum servis armatis
8 defendit.

Names

Catilina, -ae m.   Catilina   Cicero, -onis m.   Cicero

Words

coniuratio, -onis f. conspiracy, plot   armo, -are, -avi, -atus   I arm
coniuratus, -i m.   conspirator, plotter

(a) Catilina ... voluerat (line 1): what **two** facts are we given here about
    Catilina?   [4]

(b) cum ... coepit (lines 1-4):
    (i)   why were Catilina's hoped dashed?   [2]
    (ii)   describe Catilina's army.   [2]
    (iii) what did Catilina begin to do?   [2]

(c) Catilina ... caperent (lines 4-5): which **three** of the following statements
    are true? Write down the letters for the ones that are correct.
            A   Catilina met with his fellow-conspirators
            B   the leaders came to Catilina's house
            C   a friend received Catilina into his house
            D   Catilina's friends met at Catilina's house
            E   the leaders of the conspiracy wished to make a plan
            F   Catilina's friend wished to make a plan   [3]

(d) duos ... necandum (lines 5-6): what plan was made?   [4]

(e) Cicero ... defendit (lines 6-8): how did Cicero save himself?   [3]

Total mark for Question 1: [20]

2   *Cicero deals effectively with the conspiracy.*

Cicero, simulatque impetum duorum hominum <u>reppulit</u>, ad senatum festinavit, ut senatoribus quid accidisset nuntiaret. in foro quoque civibus convocatis dixit Catilinam mortem suam et aliorum senatorum cupere. et cives et senatores eum hortati sunt ut <u>coniuratos</u> vinceret. Catilina, urbe relicta, ad exercitum suum contendit. ubi quidam Ciceroni epistulas, a ducibus <u>coniurationis</u> scriptas, tradidit, ille satis <u>argumenti</u> iam habebat ut duces raperet. senatores rogavit quid de illis facere deberet. alii eos in <u>carcerem</u> iaciendos esse, alii necandos clamaverunt. tandem Cicero invitus eos interfici iussit.

Words

repello, -ere, reppuli	I beat off, repulse
coniuratus, -i m.	conspirator
coniuratio, -onis f.	conspiracy, plot
argumentum, -i n.	proof, evidence
carcer, -eris m.	prison

Total mark for Question 2: [30]

2   ***Paris and the beauty contest***

1   *The goddess Discord causes a fight among the goddesses.*

1   ubi ceteri dei cenam consumebant, Discordia, quae irata erat quod ad
2   cenam non invitata erat, inter deas subito apparuit. <u>malum</u> <u>aureum</u>
3   tenebat.
4   'dea,' inquit, 'quae pulcherrima omnium est, hoc <u>malum</u> habere
5   poterit.'
6   Discordia statim discessit. deae, quod omnes <u>malum</u> cupiebant,
7   mox pugnare coeperunt.
8   'nolite pugnare,' clamavit Iuppiter. 'nobis necesse est <u>certamen</u>
9   habere. iudex erit Paris, filius regis Troiae. Paris est iuvenis
10   pulcherrimus, cui nos dei favemus.'

Names

Discordia, -ae f.	Discord	*Iuppiter, Iovis* m.	Jupiter
Paris, -idis m.	Paris	*Troia, -ae* f.	Troy (a city)

Words

malum, -i n.	apple
aureus, -a, -um	golden
certamen, -inis n.	contest

(a) *ubi ... tenebat* (lines 1-3):
    (i)   what were all the other gods apart from Discord doing?   [1]
    (ii)   which **three** of the following statements are true? Write down the letters for the ones that are correct.
        A Discord was angry
        B the rest of the gods were angry
        C Discord had not invited the other gods to the dinner
        D Discord had not been invited to the dinner
        E Discord suddenly appeared among the goddesses
        F Discord suddenly appeared among the gods   [3]
    (iii) why do you think the other gods might have been suprised when they saw Discord? Give **two** reasons.   [2]

(b) *dea ... poterit* (lines 4-5): what did Discord say the golden apple was for?   [2]

(c) *Discordia ... coeperunt* (lines 6-7):
    (i)   what did Discord do?   [2]
    (ii)   what did the goddesses do?   [2]
    (iii) why was this?   [2]

(d) *nolite ... Iuppiter* (line 8): what order did Jupiter give to the goddesses?   [2]

(e) *nobis ... favemus* (lines 8-10): explain in detail how Jupiter planned to end the fight.   [4]

Total mark for Question 1: [20]

2 *Paris is called on to judge the goddesses Juno, Minerva and Venus.*

Iuppiter Mercurium misit, qui Paridi nuntiaret quid faciendum esset. Paris, simulac verba Mercurii audivit, tres deas conspexit. cum omnes pulcherrimae essent, Paris timebat ne duae victae se punirent. dum eas spectat, primum Iuno ei dixit: 'si me legeris, tibi magnum regnum dabo.' deinde Minerva promisit se maximam in bello <u>virtutem</u> ei daturam esse. <u>denique</u> Venus, 'sicut me,' inquit, 'pulcherrimam deam leges, tu uxorem habebis, quae longe pulchrior est quam ceterae feminae.'

144

quibus auditis Paris Venerem legit. illa eum hortata est ut Spartam iter faceret; ibi enim habitabat Helena, pulcherrima omnium feminarum.

Names

Mercurius, -i m.	Mercury (a god)	*Iuno, -onis* f.	Juno
Minerva, -ae f.	Minerva	*Venus, -eris* f.	Venus
Sparta, -ae f.	Sparta (a city)	*Helena, -ae* f.	Helen

Words

virtus, -utis f.	courage
denique	finally

Total mark for Question 2: [30]

3   The story of Titus Latinius

1   *The Romans insult the gods.*

1 Romani <u>ludos</u> magnos in <u>circo</u> paraverant. prima luce, priusquam
2 <u>ludi</u> coepti sunt, civis quidam servum suum per medium <u>circum</u> egit,
3 eum ferociter <u>verberans</u>. hoc erat <u>sacrilegium</u>, quod <u>ludi</u> deis sacri
4 erant: necesse erat Romanis deos orare, ne irati essent. Romani tamen
5 hoc non fecerunt. paucis postea diebus civis notus, Latinius nomine,
6 <u>somnium</u> habuit: Iuppiter ei visus est dicere <u>ludos</u> sibi non placuisse.

Names

Latinius m.	(Titus) Latinius	*Iuppiter, Iovis* m. Jupiter

Words

ludi, -orum m pl.	games (held in honour of the gods)
circus, -i m.	circus (a sports arena)
verbero, -are	I beat
sacrilegium, -i n.	an insult to the gods
somnium, -i n.	dream

(a) *Romani ... paraverant* (line 1): what had the Romans been doing?   [3]

(b) *prima ... verberans* (lines 1-3): which **four** of the following statements are true? Write down the letters for the ones that are correct.

    A it was dawn
    B at first there was some light
    C the games had started
    D the games had not yet started
    E a citizen was beating a slave
    F a slave was beating a citizen
    G the slave was chasing the citizen through the circus
    H the citizen was chasing the slave through the circus   [4]

(c) *hoc ... essent* (lines 3-4):
    (i)   why was what had happened an insult to the gods?   [2]
    (ii) what should the Romans have done?   [3]

(d) *Romani ... fecerunt* (lines 4-5): what do you think *hoc* refers to?   [1]

(e) *paucis ... placuisse* (lines 5-6):
    (i)   when did the final episode in this section happen?   [2]
    (ii) who was Latinius?   [1]
    (iii) what exactly was his dream?   [4]

Total mark for Question 1: [20]

2   *Latinius persuades the senators to satisfy the gods.*

'ad senatores i,' inquit Iuppiter; 'haec verba eis nuntia: dei irati sunt. novi <u>ludi</u> parandi sunt, maiores quam antea. nisi hoc fecerint, urbs poenas dabit.'

    postridie Latinius, quamquam senatoribus nuntiare volebat id quod audiverat, timebat ne illi se <u>deriderent</u>. domi igitur mansit. illa nocte filius eius subito mortuus est. Latinius, eodem deo in <u>somnio</u> iterum viso, adhuc <u>haesitabat</u>. mox ipse <u>morbum</u> dirum patiebatur. tandem vix vivus ad senatum portatus est. ibi senatores hortatus est ut <u>ludos</u> iterum pararent. simulac consenserunt, Latinius domum ambulavit laetissimus.

Words

ludi, -orum m pl.	games (held in honour of the gods)	*somnium, -i* n.	dream
derideo, -ere	I laugh at	*haesito, -are*	I hesitate
		morbus, -i m.	illness

Total mark for Question 2: [30]

4 How Coriolanus saved his honour

1 *Marcius wins glory and a new name during a war against the Volsci.*

1 Romani Coriolos, urbem Volscorum, oppugnabant. inter milites erat
2 iuvenis, Marcius nomine. cum manus hominum e portis urbis egressa
3 esset, ut Romanos oppugnaret, Marcius non solum impetum eorum
4 retudit, sed etiam per portas apertas paucis cum comitibus ferociter
5 cucurrit, caedeque in magna parte urbis facta, aedificia incendit. cives
6 tantum clamorem sustulerunt, ut ceteri Romani in urbem contenderent.
7 urbe capta, Marcius propter virtutem nomen Coriolanum accepit.

Names

Corioli, -orum m pl.   Corioli (a town)
Volsci, -orum m pl.   the Volsci (a race of people living south of Rome)
Marcius, -i m.   Marcius
Coriolanus, -i m.   Coriolanus

Words

retundo, -ere, -tudi   I beat back
caedes, -is f.   slaughter
virtus, -utis f.   courage

(a) *Romani ... oppugnabant* (line 1): what were the Romans doing?   [2]

(b) *inter ... nomine* (lines 1-2): give **two** details about Marcius.   [2]

(c) *cum ... incendit* (lines 2-5):
   (i)   *manus hominum*: were these Romans or men from Corioli?   [1]
   (ii)   what did these men do?   [2]
   (iii)   what was their purpose?   [1]
   (iv)   what happened to the men?   [1]
   (v)   which **four** of the following statements are true? Write down the
letters for the ones that are correct.
      A   the band of men ran through the gates into the city
      B   Marcius ran through the gates into the city
      C   the gates were open
      D   Marcius was alone
      E   Marcius killed many men
      F   the men of Corioli killed many Romans
      G   the slaughter was in a large part of the city
      H   the buildings set on fire were in a large part of the city   [4]

(d) *cives ... contenderent* (lines 5-6):
    (i)   what did the citizens of Corioli do?   [1]
    (ii)   what happened as a result of this?   [3]

(e) *urbe ... accepit* (line 7):
    (i)   what happened to the city?   [1]
    (ii)   how did the Romans show their gratitude to Marcius?   [2]

Total mark for Question 1: [20]

2   *Coriolanus first betrays Rome, and then saves it.*

paucis annis postea erat Romae <u>inopia</u> frumenti. multi senatores, inter quos primus erat Coriolanus, <u>plebi</u> frumentum dare nolebant. cives tam irati erant ut Coriolanum ex urbe <u>expellerent</u>. ille, postquam ad Volscos fugit, eis persuasit ut bellum Romanis <u>inferrent</u>. Coriolano duce, copias Romanas saepe vicerunt. tandem, multis aliis urbibus captis, exercitus Volscorum ad portas Romae ipsius pervenit. civibus desperantibus, uxor et mater Coriolani cum duobus filiis ad castra hostium contenderunt. priusquam Coriolanus eas <u>complecteretur</u>, mater eum rogavit utrum ad filium an ad hostem venisset. his verbis victus, Coriolanus exercitum ab urbe duxit.

Words

inopia, -ae f.	shortage
plebs, -is f.	the lower classes (of citizens)
expello, -ere	I drive out
inferro, -ferre (+ dat.)	I declare (war) (on)
complector, -i	I embrace

Total mark for Question 2: [30]

5 The Fabii take on the Etruscan army

1 Caeso Fabius promises to defend Rome against Veii.

```
1  Romani  longum  bellum  gerebant contra gentes finitimas, quae
2  Romam  vincere  volebant. inter eas Veientes maximum periculum
3  faciebant; agros enim Romanos saepe ingressi sunt, ut frumentum
4  delerent. cum tot hostes essent, Caeso Fabius consul senatoribus haec
5  dixit: 'gens mea exercitum contra Veientes praebere vult; cives Romani
6  alias copias contra ceteros hostes parare possunt.' senatores ei gratias
7  egerunt. hoc cognito populus Romanus Fabium laudavit.
```

Names

Veientes, -um m pl.

the people of Veii (an Etruscan city near Rome)

Caeso Fabius, Caesonis Fabii, m.

Caeso Fabius

Words

finitimus, -a, -um   neighbouring

(a) Romani ... volebant (lines 1-2):
    (i)   what were the Romans doing? [4]
    (ii) what are we told about the gentes finitimas? [3]

(b) inter ... delerent (lines 2-4): which **three** of the following statements are true? Write down the letters for the ones that are correct.
        A the people of Veii caused most trouble among the races
        B the people of Veii caused most trouble to the Romans
        C the Romans often invaded the territory of Veii
        D the people of Veii often invaded Roman territory
        E they invaded to destroy the food supply
        F they invaded because their food supply was destroyed [3]

(c) cum ... dixit (lines 4-5):
    (i)   why did Caeso Fabius address the senators? [2]
    (ii) who was Fabius? [1]

(d) *gens ... possunt* (lines 5-6):
   (i)   which is the best translation of *gens mea* here?
       A my race
       B my family
       C my tribe
       D my people   [1]

   (ii) what did *gens mea* wish to provide?   [2]
   (iii) what did Fabius suggest the citizens of Rome should do?   [3]

(e) *hoc ... laudavit* (line 7): when did the Roman people praise Fabius? [1]

Total mark for Question 1: [20]

2   *Fabius' plan fails.*

postridie <u>trecenti</u> sex Fabii per vias urbis plenas civium gaudentium contenderunt. consule duce ex urbe profecti, ad flumen latum venerunt. castris hic positis, multos dies Fabii impetus in agros Veientum faciebant, nonnullosque homines etiam interficiebant. tandem Veientes novum consilium ceperunt: <u>pecora</u> in agros prope castra Fabiorum ducebant, ut illi ea capere conarentur. mox Fabii tam audaces erant ut procul a castris progrederentur. deinde Veientes insidias paraverunt: Fabios <u>pecora</u> per agros sequentes subito multa milia militum <u>undique</u> oppugnaverunt. Fabii, quamquam fortissime restiterunt, omnes necati sunt.

Names

Fabii, -orum m pl.   members of the *gens Fabia*

Words

trecenti, -ae, -a   three hundred
pecora, -um n pl.   cattle
undique   from all sides

Total mark for Question 2: [30]

6 The myth of Prometheus

1 Prometheus helps mankind to cheat the gods.

1 Iuppiter, qui erat rex deorum, homines creavit; sacrificia enim ab eis
2 accipere volebat. Prometheus eum adiuvit. cum tamen homines primum
3 sacrificium facerent, Prometheus eis persuasit ut deis darent victimae
4 ossa, adipe involuta. 'si id feceritis,' inquit, 'vos ipsi carnem consumere
5 poteritis.' quamquam hoc hominibus placebat, Iuppiter, simulatque
6 intellexit quid accidisset, iratissimus erat. ceteris deis convocatis
7 clamavit 'homines puniendi sunt.' feminas igitur creavit, ut viri semper
8 poenas darent.

Names

Iuppiter, Iovis m.	Jupiter
Prometheus, -i m.	Prometheus

Words

creo, -are, -avi	I create
sacrificium, -i n.	sacrifice
victima, -ae f.	victim (sacrificial animal)
os, ossis n.	bone
adeps, -ipis m.	fat
involvo, -ere, -volvi, -volutus	I wrap
caro, -nis f.	meat

(a) *Iuppiter ... volebat* (lines 1-2):
    (i)   who was Jupiter? [2]
    (ii) what did he do? [1]
    (iii) why did he do this? [2]

(b) Which is the correct translation of *Prometheus eum adiuvit* (line 2)?
    A Prometheus heard him
    B Prometheus approached him
    C Prometheus helped him
    D Prometheus joined him [1]

(c) *cum ... involuta* (lines 2-4):
    (i)   when did Prometheus suggest that men should deceive the
          gods? [2]
    (ii) what was the deception? [4]

(d) *si ... erat* (lines 4-6): explain why men were pleased, but Jupiter was very angry when he learnt of Prometheus' advice.   [2]

(e) *ceteris ... sunt* (lines 6-7): which **three** of the following statements are true? Write down the letters for the ones that are correct.
   A   Jupiter called the rest of the gods together
   B   the rest of the gods called out
   C   Jupiter shouted
   D   the rest of the gods shouted
   E   'men are punishing us,' was shouted
   F   'men must be punished,' was shouted   [3]

(f) *feminas ... darent* (lines 7-8):
   (i)   what was the punishment?   [2]
   (ii) suggest a reason why *viri* is used here for 'men', rather than *homines*.   [1]

Total mark for Question 1: [20]

2   *Prometheus is punished for helping mankind again by giving them fire.*

Prometheus erat tristis, quod homines sine igni vitam miserrimam habebant. Iuppiter tamen, qui cognoverat Prometheum homines iterum adiuvare velle, ei imperavit ne ignem eis daret. Prometheus, quamquam iram Iovis timebat, hominibus ignem dedit, quo cibum <u>coquerent</u>. illi iam multo laetiores erant. Iuppiter autem, simulatque intellexit quid Prometheus fecisset, tam iratus erat, ut eum punire constitueret. Prometheus, captus inque montes ductus, ad <u>rupem</u> <u>ligatus est</u>. <u>cotidie</u> <u>iecur</u> ab ingenti <u>aquila</u> consumebatur; <u>noctu</u> <u>iecur</u> reficiebatur. ita, quod benignus fuerat, plurimos annos puniebatur.

Words

coquo, -ere	I cook
rupes, -is f.	rock
ligo, -are, -avi, -atus	I tie
cotidie	every day
iecur, -oris n.	liver
aquila, -ae f.	eagle
noctu	at night

Total mark for Question 2: [30]

7 Actaeon and Diana

1 *The hunter Actaeon takes a wrong turning.*

1 Actaeon in silva cum amicis canibusque <u>venari</u> solebat. olim
2 postquam multos <u>cervos</u> hastis necaverunt, Actaeon comitibus
3 persuasit ut domum <u>cervos</u> mortuos portarent; ipse enim, quod sol
4 adhuc in medio caelo erat, per silvam cum canibus suis diutius
5 ambulare volebat. paucas horas progressus, primum voces audivit,
6 deinde magnam <u>speluncam</u> conspexit, in qua puellae pulcherrimae
7 circum feminam etiam pulchriorem sedebant. illa prope <u>fontem</u> sine
8 vestimentis stabat.

Names

Actaeon, -onis m.   Actaeon

Words

venor, -ari	I hunt
cervus, -i m.	stag
spelunca, -ae f.	cave
fons, fontis m.	spring

(a) *Actaeon ... solebat* (line 1):
  (i) which is the correct translation of *Actaeon venari solebat*?
       A Actaeon hunted when it was sunny
       B Actaeon hunted alone
       C Actaeon was accustomed to go hunting
       D Actaeon was alone when hunting   [1]
  (ii) who accompanied him?   [2]

(b) *olim ... portarent* (lines 1-3):
  (i) what was the result of the hunting?   [2]
  (ii) what task did Actaeon give to the others?   [2]

(c) *ipse ... volebat* (lines 3-5):
  (i) what did Actaeon wish to do?   [4]
  (ii) what time of day was it?   [1]

(d) *paucas ... sedebant* (lines 5-7):
  (i) for how long did Actaeon walk?   [2]

(ii) which **four** of the following statements are true? Write down the letters for the ones that are correct.

        A first Actaeon heard voices
        B Actaeon heard the first voices
        C then Actaeon saw a large cave
        D some girls were standing in the cave
        E the girls were very beautiful
        F there was a woman sitting apart from the girls
        G the girls were more beautiful than the woman
        H the woman was more beautiful than the girls   [4]

(e) *illa ... stabat* (lines 7-8):
    (i)   to which person does *illa* refer?   [1]
    (ii)   why might this person have been embarrassed?   [1]

Total mark for Question 1: [20]

2   *Actaeon pays with his life for his mistake.*

femina, quam Actaeon conspexerat, erat dea Diana, quae <u>venatione</u> confecta <u>cotidie</u> cum ancillis in illam <u>speluncam</u> ire solebat. illae, simulac virum conspexerunt, ad dominam celandam festinaverunt; quae, cupiens eum punire, nihil aliud nisi aquam habebat, quam iaceret. hac in vultum iuvenis iacta, eum <u>exsecrata est</u>.

'nunc,' inquit, 'omnibus nuntiare conaberis te deam sine vestimentis vidisse – si poteris! num iam sic ad canes tuos redire audebis?'

Actaeon <u>cornua</u> <u>cervi</u> in capite <u>crescere</u> sensit. mox quattuor pedes habebat. perterritus e <u>spelunca</u> cucurrit, celerius quam antea. canibus suis statim necatus est.

Name

Diana, -ae f.	Diana (goddess of hunting)

Words

venatio, -onis f.	hunt, hunting
cotidie	every day
spelunca, -ae f.	cave
exsecror, -ari, -atus sum	I curse
cornu,-us n.	horn
cervus, -i m.	stag
cresco, -ere	I grow

Total mark for Question 2: [30]

8 Spartacus

1 Spartacus gathers an army.

1 Spartacus erat <u>gladiator</u> fortis feroxque. in <u>ludo</u> prope Capuam gladio
2 atque hasta pugnare docebatur. cum tamen hanc vitam odisset, ira
3 motus <u>lanistam</u> crudelem necavit. ceteris <u>gladiatoribus</u> eum
4 sequentibus, e <u>ludo</u> effugit. hanc manum hominum <u>servitio</u> liberatorum
5 per agros circumiacentes ducere coepit. in omnibus locis servis
6 persuadere conatus est, ut dominos relinquerent. servi, quod labor in
7 agris durissimus erat, verbis Spartaci auditis laetissime paruerunt.

Names

Spartacus, -i m.	Spartacus
Capua, -aei f.	Capua (a city in the south of Italy)

Words

gladiator, -oris m.	gladiator
ludus, -i m.	gladiatorial training school
lanista, -ae m.	trainer
servitium, -i n.	slavery

(a) *Spartacus ... feroxque* (line 1): how is the gladiator, Spartacus,
   described?   [2]

(b) *in ludo ... docebatur* (lines 1-2): what happened in the school?   [4]

(c) *cum ... necavit* (lines 2-3): which **three** of the following statements are
   true? Write down the letters for the ones that are correct.
       A Spartacus hated being a gladiator
       B Spartacus liked his life
       C Spartacus moved angrily
       D Spartacus acted out of anger
       E Spartacus killed the cruel trainer
       F Spartacus cruelly killed the trainer   [3]

(d) *ceteris ... effugit* (lines 3-4):
     (i)   what did Spartacus do?   [1]
     (ii) how do we know that the other gladiators approved of his
         action?   [1]

(e) *hanc ... coepit* (lines 4-5):
  - (i) write down and translate the word that describes the men. [2]
  - (ii) where did Spartacus lead the men? [2]

(f) *in omnibus ... relinquerent* (lines 5-6): how did Spartacus try to increase his numbers? [4]

(g) *servi ... paruerunt* (lines 6-7): look at the following statements based on these words:
  - (i) the slaves were very tough
  - (ii) the slaves were very happy
  - (iii) the slaves worked on the land
  - (iv) the land was very hard
  - (v) the slaves heard Spartacus' words
  - (vi) Spartacus heard the slaves' voices

Which **three** of the above statements are true?
  A (i), (v) and (vi)
  B (ii), (iii) and (v)
  C (i), (ii) and (iv)
  D (ii), (iv) and (vi) [1]

Total mark for Question 1: [20]

2   *At first Spartacus is successful, but in the end he fails.*

Spartacus, postquam servos ad se vocare coepit, brevi tempore magnam turbam virorum feminarumque circum se habebat. plurimi horum nec gladium neque hastam umquam tenuerant. Spartacus, cum timeret ne Romani exercitum contra se mitterent, amicis imperavit ut omnes servos pugnare docerent. eodem tempore ei qui poterant novos gladios hastasque fecerunt. mox tantus exercitus armatorum paratus erat pro libertate pugnare, ut primus exercitus, quem Romani miserunt, facile vinceretur. deinde tamen alter maiorque exercitus Romanus, ab imperatore peritiore ductus, pervenit. hic exercitus copias Spartaci superavit; qui ipse necatus est.

Words

armati, -orum m.pl.	armed men
libertas, -atis f.	freedom
peritus, -a, -um	experienced

Total mark for Question 2: [30]

9 The Emperor Caligula

1 *Caligula's love life.*

1 Caligula multas feminas amabat. saepe, senatoribus ad cenam
2 invitatis, si uxor cuiusdam ei placebat, marito imperavit ut eam
3 repudiaret; deinde ipse eam amare poterat. etiam sororem suam,
4 Drusillam, adeo amabat ut, postquam mortua est, maximos honores ei
5 daret. inter tot feminas una, Caesonia nomine, amorem imperatoris diu
6 accipiebat. Caligula eam, quamquam nec pulchra neque iuvenis erat,
7 iamque tres filias ex alio viro habebat, tandem in matrimonium duxit.

Names

Caligula, -ae m.	Caligula
Drusilla, -ae f.	Drusilla
Caesonia, -ae f.	Caesonia

Words

repudio, -are, -avi	I divorce
honos, -oris m.	honour
matrimonium, -i n.	marriage

(a) *Caligula ... amabat* (line 1): what are we told about Caligula?　　[3]

(b) *saepe ... poterat* (lines 1-3): which **four** of the following statements are
　　true? Write down the letters for the ones that are correct.
　　　　A Caligula invited senators to dinner
　　　　B senators invited Caligula to dinner
　　　　C someone liked Caligula's wife
　　　　D a senator's wife liked Caligula
　　　　E Caligula liked a senator's wife
　　　　F Caligula ordered the senator to divorce his wife
　　　　G the senator ordered his wife to divorce him
　　　　H Caligula could then have an affair with the woman　　[4]

(c) *etiam ... daret* (lines 3-5):
　　(i)　who was Drusilla?　　[1]
　　(ii)　how did Caligula show his great passion for her?　　[4]

(d) *inter ... accipiebat* (lines 5-6): what was special about Caesonia?　　[4]

(e) *Caligula ... duxit* (lines 6-7): what reasons might Caligula have had for not marrying Caesonia? [4]

Total mark for Question 1: [20]

2   *The death of Caligula.*

Caligula, per quattuor annos in quibus imperium tenebat, tot homines occidit ut cives magnopere timerent, ne ira imperatoris contra se verteretur. is multos necavit ut pecuniam eorum raperet, alios quod eum non satis laudaverant, ceteros nulla alia causa quam quod optimi viri erant. senatores, qui eum maxime oderant, tandem duobus militibus persuaserunt ut imperatorem gladiis <u>percuterent</u>. milites, dum imperatorem necant, senem conspexerunt post ianuam celatum. illum quoque, quod viderat quid accidisset, necare paraverunt. tum milites senem <u>agnoverunt</u>: erat Claudius, <u>patruus</u> Caligulae. milites eum imperatorem <u>proximum</u> futurum esse statim nuntiaverunt.

Name

Claudius, -i m.   Claudius

Words

percutio, -ere   I strike
agnosco, -ere, -novi   I recognise
patruus, -i m.   uncle
proximus, -a, -um   next

Total mark for Question 2: [30]

158

10 *The story of Arachne*

1 *Arachne challenges the goddess Minerva to a weaving contest.*

1 Arachne erat filia pauperis. tantam artem autem <u>lanificii</u> ostendebat ut
2 multi venirent ad eam spectandam. aliquis dixit se credere Arachnen a
3 Minerva doctam esse. his verbis auditis, Arachne, 'noli id credere,'
4 inquit. 'ipsa me omnia docui. ars mea multo melior est quam Minervae.
5 si illa mecum <u>certaverit</u>, tu mox intelleges deam a me multa <u>discere</u>
6 posse.' Minerva, simulatque hoc cognovit, iratissima erat. statim
7 constituit eam puniendam esse.

Names

Arachne, -es (acc.-*en*) f.	Arachne
Minerva, -ae f.	Minerva (goddess of crafts)

Words

lanificium, -i n.	spinning and weaving
certo, -are, -avi	I have a contest
disco, -ere	I learn

(a) *Arachne ... pauperis* (line 1): who was Arachne? [2]

(b) *tantam ... spectandam* (lines 1-2):
    (i)   why was Arachne special? [2]
    (ii) which is the correct translation of *ad eam spectandam*?
         A they looked at her
         B they were watching for her
         C to watch her
         D to that show [1]

(c) *aliquis ... esse* (lines 2-3):
    (i)   what belief did someone have about Arachne? [2]
    (ii) what did this suggest about Arachne's skill? [1]

(d) *his ... docui* (lines 3-4): which **three** of the following statements are
true? Write down the letters for the ones that are correct.
         A Arachne heard what was said
         B Minerva heard what was said
         C Arachne told the speaker not to believe what was said
         D Arachne said she did not believe what was said
         E Arachne said Minerva had taught her everything
         F Arachne said she was self-taught [3]

(e) *ars ... Minervae* (line 4): what comparison did Arachne make?　　　[3]

(f) *si ... posse* (lines 5-6):
　　(i)　what did Arachne suggest she wanted to happen?　　　[2]
　　(ii)　what did she think would be the result of this?　　　[2]

(g) *Minerva ... esse* (lines 6-7):
　　(i)　how did Minerva feel when she found this out?　　　[1]
　　(ii)　what did she decide should be done?　　　[1]

Total mark for Question 1: [20]

2　*Arachne pays for her arrogance.*

Minerva vestimenta <u>anilia</u> gerebat. domum Arachnes ingressa, lente sicut <u>anus</u> locuta est.

'meum consilium tibi accipiendum est. si <u>veniam</u> deae pro verbis tuis rogaveris, illa <u>veniam</u> dabit.'

Arachne, 'audesne', inquit, 'ad me venire sic annis confecta? tua verba stulta numquam mihi persuadebunt. cur dea ipsa ad <u>certandum</u> non venit?'

Minerva, vestimentis <u>mutatis</u>, statim respondit: 'ego veni!'

et femina et dea ad <u>telas</u> sedebant. <u>texere</u> coeperunt. multas post horas <u>aulaea</u> confecta inspexerunt: aeque pulchra erant. dea tam irata erat ut Arachnen in <u>araneam</u> mutaret.

'sic <u>texere</u> semper poteris,' dixit ridens.

Words

anilis, -is, -e	of an old woman
anus, -us f.	old woman
venia, -ae f.	forgiveness
certo, -are	I have a contest
muto, -are	I change
tela, -ae f.	loom
texo, -ere	I weave
aulaeum, -i n.	tapestry
aranea, -ae f.	spider

Total mark for Question 2: [30]